FAITH LESSONS

ON THE prophets & KINGS of ISRAEL

PARTICIPANT'S GUIDE

Also Available from Ray Vander Laan

Video and Group Resources

Faith Lessons on the Death and Resurrection of the Messiah
Faith Lessons on the Life and Ministry of the Messiah
Faith Lessons on the Promised Land

Book and Audiocassette

Echoes of His Presence

FAITH LESSONS
ON THE prophets
& KINGS OF ISRAEL

PARTICIPANT'S GUIDE

Ray Vander Laan

with
Stephen and Amanda Sorenson

ZondervanPublishingHouse
Grand Rapids, Michigan

A Division of HarperCollinsPublishers

Faith Lessons on the Prophets and Kings of Israel Participant's Guide
Copyright © 1999 by Ray Vander Laan

Requests for information should be addressed to:

ZondervanPublishingHouse
Grand Rapids, Michigan 49530

ISBN 0-310-67897-8

Interior design by Sherri Hoffman

Printed in the United States of America

05 06 07 08 09 10 /❖DC/ 19 18 17 16 15 14 13 12

contents

Introduction

Because God speaks to us through the Scriptures, studying them is a rewarding experience. The inspired human authors of the Bible, as well as those to whom the words were originally given, were primarily Jews living in the Near East. God's words and actions spoke to them with such power, clarity, and purpose that they wrote them down and carefully preserved them as an authoritative body of literature.

God's use of human servants in revealing Himself resulted in writings that clearly bear the stamp of time and place. The message of the Scriptures is, of course, eternal and unchanging—but the circumstances and conditions of the people of the Bible are unique to their times. Consequently, we most clearly understand God's truth when we know the cultural context within which He spoke and acted and the perception of the people with whom He communicated. This does not mean that God's revelation is unclear if we don't know the cultural context. Rather, by learning how to think and approach life as Abraham, Moses, Ruth, Esther, and Paul did, modern Christians will deepen their appreciation of God's Word. To fully apply the message of the Bible, we must enter the world of the Hebrews and familiarize ourselves with their culture.

That is the purpose of this study. The events and characters of the Bible are presented in their original settings. Although the videos offer the latest archaeological research, this series is not intended to be a definitive cultural and geographical study of the lands of the Bible. No original scientific discoveries are revealed here. The purpose of this study is to help us better understand God's revealed mission for our lives by enabling us to hear and see His words in their original context.

understanding the world of the Hebrews

More than 3,800 years ago, God spoke to His servant Abraham: "Go, walk through the length and breadth of the land, for I am giving it to you" (Genesis 13:17). From the outset, God's choice of a Hebrew nomad to begin His plan of salvation (that is still unfolding) was linked to the selection of a specific land where His redemptive work would begin. The nature of God's covenant relationship with His people demanded a place where their faith could be exercised and displayed to all nations so that the world would know of *Yahweh,* the true and faithful God. God showed the same care in preparing a land for His chosen people as He did in preparing a people to live in that land. For us to fully understand God's plan and purpose for His people, we must first understand the nature of the place He selected for them.

By New Testament times, the Jewish people had been removed from the Promised Land by the Babylonians due to Israel's failure to live obediently before God (Jeremiah 25:4–11). The exile lasted seventy years, but its impact upon God's people was astounding. New patterns of worship developed, and scribes and experts in God's law shaped the new commitment to be faithful to Him. The prophets predicted the appearance of a Messiah like King David who would revive the kingdom of the Hebrew people.

But the Promised Land was now home to many other groups of people whose religious practices, moral values, and lifestyles conflicted with those of the Jews. Living as God's witnesses took on added difficulty as Greek, Roman, and Samaritan worldviews mingled with that of the Israelites. The Promised Land was divided between kings and governors, usually under the authority of one foreign empire or another. But the mission of God's people did not change. They were still to live *so that the world would know that their God was the true God.* And the land continued to provide them opportunity to encounter the world that desperately needed to know this reality.

The Promised Land was the arena within which God's people were to serve Him faithfully as the world watched. The land God chose for His people was on the crossroads of the world. A major trade route, the Via Maris, ran through it. God intended for the Israelites to take control of the cities along this route and thereby exert influence on the nations around them. Through their righteous living, the Hebrews were to reveal the one true God, *Yahweh,* to the world. They failed to accomplish this mission, however, because of their unfaithfulness.

Western Christianity tends to spiritualize the concept of the Promised Land as it is presented in the Bible. Instead of seeing it as a crossroads from which to influence the world, modern Christians view it as a distant, heavenly city, a glorious "Canaan" toward which we are traveling as we ignore the world around us. We are focused on the destination, not the journey. We have unconsciously separated our walk with God from our responsibility to the world in which He has placed us. In one sense, our earthly experience is simply preparation for an eternity in the "promised land." Preoccupation with this idea, however, distorts the mission God has set for us.

Living by faith is not a vague, otherworldly experience; rather, it is being faithful to God right now, in the place and time in which He has put us. This truth is emphasized by God's choice of Canaan, a crossroads of the ancient world, as the Promised Land for the Israelites. God wants His people in the game, not on the bench. Our mission, as Christians today, is the same one He gave to the Israelites. We are to live obediently *within* the world so that through us *the world may know that our God is the one true God.*

The Assumptions of Biblical Writers

Biblical writers assumed that their readers were familiar with Near Eastern geography. The geography of Canaan shaped the culture of the people living there. Their settlements began near sources of water and food. Climate and raw materials shaped their choice of occupation, dress, weapons, diet, and even artistic expression. As their cities grew, they interacted politically. Trade developed, and trade routes were established.

During New Testament times, the Promised Land was called Palestine or Judea. *Judea,* (which means "Jewish") technically referred to the land that had been the nation of Judah. Because of the influence that the people of Judea had over the rest of the land, the land itself was called Judea. The Romans divided the land into several provinces, including Judea, Samaria, and Galilee (the three main divisions during Jesus' time); Gaulanitis, the Decapolis, and Perea (east of the Jordan River); and Idumaea (Edom) and Nabatea (in the south). These further divisions of Israel added to the rich historical and cultural background God prepared for the coming of Jesus and the beginning of His church.

Today the names *Israel* and *Palestine* are often used to designate the land God gave to Abraham. Both terms are politically charged. *Palestine* is used by the Arabs living in the central part of the country, while *Israel* is used by the Jews to indicate the State of Israel. In this study, *Israel* is used in the biblical sense. This choice does not indicate a political statement regarding the current struggle in the Middle East but instead is chosen to best reflect the biblical designation for the land.

Unfortunately, many Christians do not have even a basic geographical knowledge of the region. This series is designed to help solve that problem. We will be studying the people and events of the Bible in their geographical and historical contexts. Once we know the *who*, *what*, and *where* of a Bible story, we will be able to understand the *why*. By deepening our understanding of God's Word, we can strengthen our relationship with God.

The biblical writers also used a language that, like all languages, is bound by culture and time. Therefore, understanding the Scriptures involves more than knowing what the words mean. We need to also understand those words from the perspective of the people who used them.

The people whom God chose as His instruments—the people to whom He revealed Himself—were Hebrews living in the Near East. These people described their world and themselves in concrete terms. Their language was one of pictures, metaphors, and examples rather than ideas, definitions, and abstractions. Whereas we might describe God as omniscient or omnipresent (knowing everything and present everywhere), a Hebrew would have preferred to describe God by saying, "The Lord is my shepherd." Thus, the Bible is filled with concrete images from Hebrew culture: God is our Father, and we are His children. God is the potter, and we are the clay. Jesus is the Lamb killed on Passover. Heaven is an oasis in the desert, and hell is the city sewage dump. The Last Judgment will be in the Eastern Gate of the heavenly Jerusalem and will include sheep and goats.

These people had an Eastern mindset rather than a Western mindset. Eastern thought emphasizes the process of learning as much or more than the end result. Whereas Westerners tend to collect information to find the right answer, Hebrew thought stresses the process of discovery as well as the answer. So as you go through this study, use it as an opportunity to deepen your understanding of who God is and to grow in your relationship with Him.

innocent blood—part 1

questions to think about

1. How do you think a historian 150 years from now would describe our culture's values and life priorities? How might that historian evaluate the current status of the battle between good and evil?

2. Today, many of us really want to "succeed" in life and will sacrifice a great deal in order to achieve personal benefits. Yet innocent people around us can be harmed by our choices. Give a few examples of how striving for personal success or gain can harm other people. You may use your own experiences or the experiences of people you know as examples.

IT'S WORTH OBSERVING...

The Struggle for Our Hearts and Minds

When the Israelites—nomad Hebrews—entered Canaan, they discovered a lush land of farmers, not shepherds. The Canaanites attributed this fertility to their god, Baal. Because people of that time thought of their gods in terms of a specific place, the Israelites wondered if their God, whom they perceived to be the God of the desert wilderness, was still their God in the vastly different land of Canaan. The Israelites were wondering, *Can Yahweh, who led us out of Egypt and through the wilderness also provide fertile crops in Canaan, or do we have to honor Baal? Or do we honor both?*

An intense spiritual battle began for the hearts and minds of God's people. Over and over again in the Old Testament, we read about the Israelites' attraction to and worship of Canaanite gods, God's disciplinary response, the people's repentance, and God's merciful forgiveness. Then the cycle would repeat itself.

By the time of Ahab and Jezebel, the fertility cults seem to have had the official sanction of Israel's leaders. Ahab, with his wife's encouragement, built a temple to Baal in his capital, Samaria. Yet, prophets like Elijah (whose name means "Yahweh is God"), Hosea, Isaiah, and Jeremiah thundered that Yahweh alone deserved the people's allegiance. It took the destruction of Israel by the Assyrians and the Babylonian captivity of Judah to convince the Israelites that there is only one omnipotent God.

The struggle to be totally committed to God is of vital importance to us today, too. We don't think of ourselves as idol worshipers, yet we struggle to serve God in every part of our lives. It is easy (and seductive) to honor self, possessions, fun, relationships, fame, money, and many other gods.

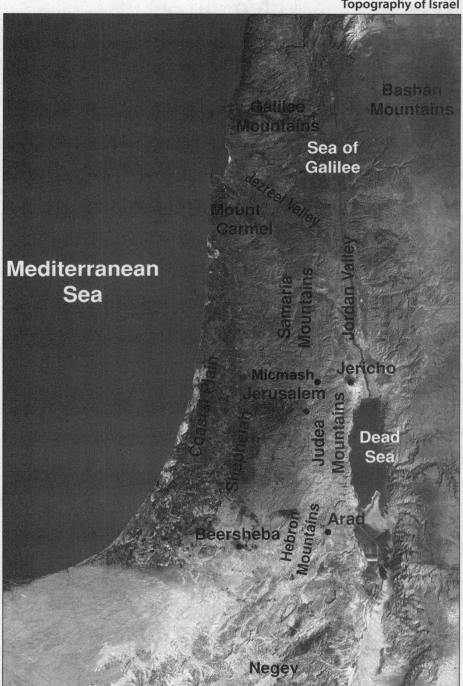

video notes

Megiddo

The Place

The Battleground for Control of the World

Baal Worship

The Battle for Good and Evil in Our Culture

video нighlights

1. Which images from the video made the most powerful impression on you? Why?

2. What thoughts are foremost in your mind as a result of seeing this video?

3. What did the Israelites and Canaanites hope to gain by sacrificing their children to Baal?

4. Do you agree that there are some remarkable similarities between our culture today and the culture of the Israelites when they worshiped both Baal and God? What similarities can you identify?

5. What was God's response to the Israelites' worship of Baal, particularly the sacrifice of infants?

6. What would God's response to child sacrifice be today?

DATA FILE

The Gods of Canaan

Baal

The earliest deity recognized by people of the ancient Near East was the creator-god, El. His mistress, the fertility goddess Asherah, supposedly gave birth to many gods, including a powerful one named Baal ("Lord"). There appears to have been only one Baal, who was manifested in lesser Baals at different times and places. Over the years, Baal became the dominant deity, and the worship of El faded away.

Baal supposedly won his dominance by defeating other deities, including the god of the sea, god of storms (also of rain, thunder, and lightning), and god of death. His victory over death was thought to be repeated each year when he returned from the land of death (the underworld) and brought rain to renew the earth's fertility.

Hebrew culture viewed the sea as evil and destructive, so Baal's promise to prevent storms and control the sea, as well as his seeming ability to produce abundant harvests, made him attractive to the Israelites. It's difficult to understand why Yahweh's people failed to see that He alone had power over these things. Possibly their desert origins led them to question God's sovereignty over fertile land. Maybe, however, the sinful pagan practices attracted them to Baal.

Baal is portrayed as a man who had the head and horns of a bull, an image similar to that in biblical accounts. His right hand (and sometimes both hands) was raised, and he held a lightning bolt that signified destruction and fertility. Baal was sometimes seated on a throne, possibly to show that he was the king or lord of the gods.

Baal worshipers appeased him by offering sacrifices, usually sheep and bulls (1 Kings 18:26). Some scholars believe that the Canaanites also sacrificed pigs and that God prohibited His people from eating pork in part to prevent this horrible cult from being established among them. (See Isaiah 65:1–5 for an example of Israel's participation in the Canaanites' pagan practices.)

(continued on page 20)

Baal Sacrifice Altar

(continued from page 19)

During times of crisis, Baal's followers sacrificed their children, apparently the firstborn of the community, in order to gain personal prosperity. The Bible calls this practice "detestable" (Deuteronomy 12:31; 18:9–10). God specifically appointed the tribe of Levi to be His special servants, in place of the firstborn of the Israelites, so they had no excuse for offering their children (Numbers 3:11–13). God hated child sacrifice, especially among those who were called to be His people.

Asherah

Asherah, in various forms and with varying names, was honored as the fertility goddess (Judges 3:7). The Bible does not actually describe her, but archaeologists have discovered figurines believed to be representations of her. She is portrayed as a nude female, sometimes pregnant, with exaggerated breasts that she holds out apparently as symbols of her fertility. The Bible indicates that she was worshiped near trees and poles, called Asherah poles (Deuteronomy 7:5; 12:2–3; 2 Kings 16:4; 17:10; Jeremiah 3:6,13; Ezekiel 6:13).

The Goddess Asherah

Asherah was worshiped in various ways, including ritual sex. Although she was believed to be Baal's mother, she was also his mistress. Pagans practiced "sympathetic magic"—that is, they believed they could influence the gods' actions by performing the behavior they wished the gods to demonstrate. Believing that the sexual union of Baal and Asherah produced fertility, their worshipers engaged in immoral sex to cause the gods to join together and thereby ensure good harvests. This practice became the basis for religious prostitution (1 Kings 14:23–24). The priest or a male community member represented Baal. The priestess or a female community member represented Asherah. Thus God's incredible gift of sexuality within the bonds of marriage was perverted and became obscene public prostitution. No wonder God's anger burned against His people and their leaders.

faith Lesson

Time for Reflection

Read the following passage of Scripture and take the next few minutes to reflect on how the message of this video applies to your life.

> This is the word that came to Jeremiah from the LORD: "Stand at the gate of the LORD's house and there proclaim this message: 'Hear the word of the LORD, all you people of Judah who come through these gates to worship the LORD. This is what the LORD Almighty, the God of Israel, says: Reform your ways and your actions, and I will let you live in this place. Do not trust in deceptive words and say, "This is the temple of the LORD, the temple of the LORD, the temple of the LORD!" If you really change your ways and your actions and deal with each other justly, if you do not oppress the alien, the fatherless or the widow and do not shed innocent blood in this place, and if you do not follow other gods to your own harm, then I will let you live in this place, in the land I gave your forefathers for ever and ever. But look, you are trusting in deceptive words that are worthless. Will you steal and murder, commit adultery and perjury, burn incense to Baal and follow other gods you have not known, and then come and stand before me in this house, which bears my Name, and say, "We are safe"—safe to do all these detestable things?'"

JEREMIAH 7:1–10

1. During King Ahab's time, the Israelites were willing to sac-
    rifice their children in a vain effort to influence Baal to give
    them good crop yields. What might you be sacrificing
    today in order to gain personal security and success? What
    do you want so badly that you are willing to sacrifice
    almost anything to obtain it?

2. It's easy to be critical of how the Israelites worshiped God
    and yet sacrificed their children to Baal, but what sinful
    patterns of belief or behavior are you holding onto? In
    what ways might you be mixing righteousness with evil?

3. In what way(s) do the lessons the Israelites learned con-
    cerning sin's attractiveness apply to your life and your
    culture?

4. How would God have you respond to the sins of your cul-
    ture and your sins?

THE ISSUES REMAIN THE SAME

Canaan's fertility cults and practices have parallels in our day. In spite of our pride in development and technology, Western culture demonstrates a growing disregard for the sacredness of human life and regularly terminates it for personal convenience. Sexuality, too, has become the goddess of much of our society—notice how it is promoted in the arts, media, music, and advertising—as if genuine success in life depends on sexual prowess and a beautiful appearance.

Human beings haven't changed much in 3,000 years. God certainly hasn't changed. He still detests the devaluation of human life, whether that occurs through abortion, oppression, ethnic cleansing, or euthanasia. He also abhors the ways in which we have perverted our sexuality.

As Christians, we are called to obey God's laws concerning sexuality and the sacredness of human life. We are also called to prophetically address the sinfulness of our culture and demonstrate by example that obeying God's laws leads to true fulfillment.

The Valley of Jezreel Viewed Across the Altar at Megiddo

DID YOU KNOW?

The word *Armageddon*, the final battle described in Revelation 16:16, is derived from the Hebrew word *Har* (that means a "hill," "mound," or "mount") and *Megiddon* (that means "Megiddo"). By choosing Megiddo to be the symbol of the end-times battle, the writer of Revelation revealed that the final battle of Armageddon will determine who will ultimately control the world. (Note: Some Christians believe the reference to Armageddon is symbolic; others believe that a literal battle for world domination will take place.)

innocent Blood — part 2

questions to Think About

1. The video we saw during our last session carried a power-ful message. Would anyone like to share some thoughts that have stayed in your mind or influenced your life since our last session together?

2. Name some people whom you think have stepped into strategic places and influenced your culture for God. What enabled them to have an influence, perhaps where other people had failed? What motivated them? What commit-ment did they make to the task? What personal price did they pay?

video notes

Tel Megiddo—Strategic Point for World Control

Baal Versus God—The Battle for Spiritual Control

The Battle in Our Culture

The Middle Eastern World

video Highlights

1. Look at the maps of Israel on page 28 and in the Data File on page 31 of your Participant's Guide. As you study the political and geographic features of this map, why do you think God chose Israel to be the land in which His plan of salvation would unfold?

2. Why was Megiddo such an important city during biblical times?

The Valley of Jezreel

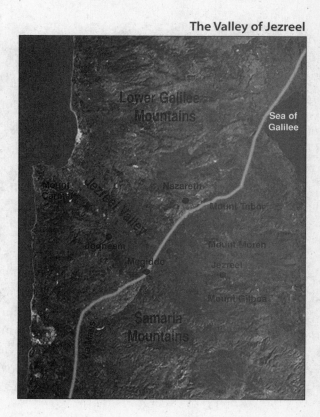

3. Why do you think Ray Vander Laan emphasized the need for Christians to occupy the "Megiddos" in our culture—the important places such as Hollywood, Wall Street, and our families—that greatly influence our culture's value system?

4. Do you agree with Ray Vander Laan that the family may be the most significant "Megiddo" of today? Why or why not?

DATA FILE

The Via Maris—Lifeline of Civilizations

Why It Was Vital

The rugged mountain ranges of Samaria, Judea, and Hebron cut through the middle of Israel, making east-west travel difficult. And the forbidding Arabian Desert to the east added to the transportation difficulties. Yet Egypt, Babylon, Assyria, and other civilizations required the exchange of vital goods. Thus, whoever controlled the road between these empires dominated international trade and exerted great influence upon other cultures.

Its Location

The road entered the Great Rift Valley from the east, near Hazor, and continued to the Sea of Galilee. Then it turned southwest into the Valley of Jezreel and cut through the ridge of Mount Carmel to reach the coastal plain. Only one of three passes through the Mount Carmel ridge provided relatively easy travel: the Iron Wadi, which was guarded by Megiddo, the most significant city in Canaan. Once past Mount Carmel, the road continued along the coast toward Egypt. The main route was several miles

inland, which enabled travelers to avoid the swamplands ~~~~
from the Judea mountains that was trapped by coastal san~~

Its Control Points

At Gezer, Hazor, and Megiddo, the Via Maris could be controlled ea~
Gezer stood where the road passed between swamplands and mountains. Hazor and Megiddo stood where the road entered mountain
passes. Megiddo guarded the most narrow pass.

Why Israel Lost Out

Because they were so afraid of the Philistines and the Canaanites, the
Israelites stayed mainly in the mountains or in the Shephelah—the
foothills between the mountains and the coastal plain. The Israelites rarely
controlled the key cities along the Via Maris, so they never exerted the
degree of influence upon world culture that God intended them to have.

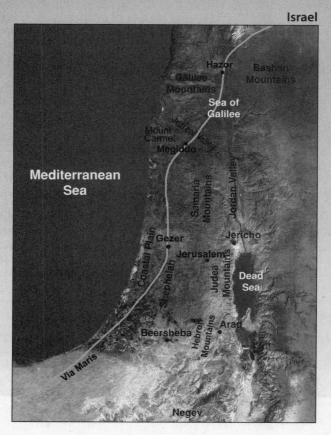

small group bible discovery

Topic A: The Battle Between Good and Evil

1. What do the following Scripture passages reveal about God's motivation for wanting His people to control and influence strategic places such as Megiddo?

   a. Isaiah 43:12

   b. 2 Kings 19:14–19

2. What did King Solomon do at Hazor, Megiddo, and Gezer—the three main cities along the Via Maris in Israel? (See 1 Kings 9:15–17.) Why?

3. Megiddo has come to represent the battle between good and evil—the battle to influence culture. Consider the ways in which that battle has been highlighted by events at Megiddo.

   a. What does the "high place" at Megiddo, where Baal was worshiped, symbolize in that battle?

   b. What great defeat for God's people took place at Megiddo? (See 2 Kings 23:29.)

c. Read Revelation 16:12–16. What is the significance of the Jewish author of Revelation locating the most decisive battle of the ages at Megiddo?

Baal Sacrifice Altar

4. Jesus, who grew up within a few miles of Megiddo and the Valley of Jezreel, made a profound impact on His culture. How did people respond to Jesus' actions? (See Matthew 15:29–31.)

Topic B: God Has His Limits

1. God loves His people and is very patient with them. Sometimes, however, He cannot tolerate any more sin and brings judgment against those who spill innocent blood. Let's briefly review some of Israel's history to see how God responded to the faithful and unfaithful kings of His people after their nation split into two parts—Israel (ten northern tribes) and Judah.

    a. Hoshea of Israel—2 Kings 17:1–6, 9–18

Actions of the King/the People	God's Response

    b. Hezekiah of Judah—2 Kings 18:1–8; 2 Chronicles 31:1

Actions of the King/the People	God's Response

    c. Manasseh, Hezekiah's son—2 Chronicles 33:1–6, 9–17

Actions of the King/the People	God's Response

d. Amon, Hezekiah's grandson—2 Chronicles 33:21–23

Actions of the King/the People	God's Response

e. Josiah, Hezekiah's great-grandson—2 Chronicles 34:1–8, 30–33; 35:25–27

Actions of the King/the People	God's Response

f. Zedekiah—2 Chronicles 36:11–20

Actions of the King/the People	God's Response

Topic C: Mixing Righteousness with Evil

Soon after entering the Promised Land, the Israelites had to choose whether they would worship the God of Israel and/or the fertility gods of the Canaanites. Often the Israelites wavered between the two: first serving God, then sacrificing to Baal and Asherah, and sometimes worshiping both.

1. Even before the Israelites crossed the Jordan River and entered the Promised Land, some of them had begun to worship the Canaanite gods. How did this come about, and what was God's response? (See Numbers 25:1–9.)

2. What do each of the following passages reveal about the impact of pagan worship practices on Israel's culture and on God's dealings with His people?

   a. Judges 10:6–16

   b. 1 Kings 10:23–24; 11:1–11

   c. 2 Chronicles 33:1–13

   d. Jeremiah 19:3–6

   e. Ezekiel 23:36–39 (Oholah and Oholibah are names for Israel and Judah)

Topic D: Worship Practices of the Canaanites

The Canaanite religions can generally be categorized as fertility cults. In addition to seeking to appease the gods through sacrifices (sometimes human), the Canaanites practiced many types of sexual perversion as part of their worship of Baal and Asherah (Ashtoreth).

1. What do the following verses reveal about the practices involved in the worship of Canaanite gods?

Reference	Worship Practices
Deuteronomy 7:5–6	
1 Kings 14:24; 22:46	
Deuteronomy 23:17–18	
Isaiah 57:5–7; Ezekiel 16:20–21	
1 Chronicles 5:25	
Hosea 4:10–14	

The High Place and Altar at Dan

2. What did the Israelites who worshiped Asherah have the audacity to do? (See 2 Kings 21:7; 23:7.)

3. What image did God use to describe Israel and Judah's pursuit of the Canaanite gods? What message was He communicating by the use of that image? (See Jeremiah 3:6–14.)

4. What image did Ezekiel use to describe Israel and Judah's worship of the Canaanite gods? (See Ezekiel 23:1–4, 35–39.)

faith Lesson

Time for Reflection

Read the following passage of Scripture and take a few minutes to consider the ways in which the battle to influence culture for God applies to you and your place in culture.

> The LORD said to me: "Son of man, will you judge Oholah and Oholibah [Israel and Judah]? Then confront them with their detestable practices, for they have committed adultery and blood is on their hands. They committed adultery with their idols; they even sacrificed their children, whom they bore to me, as food for them. They have also done this to me: At that same time they defiled my sanctuary and desecrated my Sabbaths. On the very day they sacrificed their children to their idols, they entered my sanctuary and desecrated it. That is what they did in my house. . . ." This is what the Sovereign LORD says: "Bring a mob against them and give them over to terror and plunder. . . . You will suffer the penalty for your lewdness and bear the consequences of your sins of idolatry. Then you will know that I am the Sovereign LORD."
>
> EZEKIEL 23:36–39, 46, 49

1. What must God do to get *your* attention so that you will know that He is God?

2. There is a spiritual battle between good and evil taking place all around you for the hearts, minds, and souls of people.

    a. Where are your allegiances in this battle?

    b. How deep are your loyalties?

    c. For which cause do you expend your efforts?

Action Points

Take a moment to review the key points you explored today. Then jot down an action step (or steps) that you will commit to this week as a result of what you have learned today.

1. Located above the Valley of Jezreel, Megiddo stood guard over the Via Maris at a key mountain pass: whoever controlled the city controlled the trade route. Within sight of that city, terrible battles took place in the Plain of Jezreel. *Today, as in ancient Israel, great spiritual battles are taking place throughout the world between the people of God and the people of evil, between the values of God and the values of Satan. They are battles for the hearts, minds, and souls of people—and the consequences are great.*

    What do you think God feels when He looks at the culture in which you live? Why?

Where is your "Megiddo"—the center of influence where God has placed you? What has God given you to accomplish there?

Can you identify another "Megiddo"—perhaps a more powerful center of influence within your culture—that God might be preparing you to influence for Him in the future?

2. *The Israelites were called to serve God, who loves innocence. But during King Ahab's reign, while they claimed to worship God, they also worshiped the evil gods of Canaan (especially Baal) and sacrificed their children for personal gain.* God strongly condemned their claim to honor Him while they engaged in such abominable practices.

Today, we face similar choices. How easy it can be to honor God, on the one hand, and yet allow sinful patterns of thought and action to remain rooted in our lives. How easy it can be to sacrifice others in order to gain personal blessing and achieve "success."

In what way(s) might you be sacrificing who God wants you to be or what He wants you to do in order to attain personal "success"?

In what ways are you actively fighting for God and His values against the forces of evil? Conversely, in what ways do your actions or motivations undermine the purity of your heart before God?

What practical steps will you take to seek purity before God and to honor Him in everything you do, say, and think?

3. *Megiddo also stands as a symbol of hope and promise.* It reminds us that the battle between good and evil is ultimately the battle for control of the world. Because of the redemptive work of Jesus Christ, those who engage in the battle against evil can take heart. For when the battle is finally over, Jesus Christ will be the victor. He will be crowned King of Kings!

As you face the battle to influence your culture—your Megiddo—for God, what frightens or threatens you?

In what ways does the certainty of Jesus' victory encourage you?

The Valley of Jezreel Viewed Across the Altar of Megiddo

AUTHOR'S RECOMMENDATION

I strongly recommend that participants read the well-written and exciting book, *Roaring Lambs: A Gentle Plan to Radically Change Your World* by Bob Briner. He believes that the Christian community has failed to participate in institutions and activities that have the greatest influence on culture. Citing extensive examples of Christians' failure to participate in movies, television, literature, and the visual arts, Bob presents an interesting proposal to encourage young Christians to pursue careers in those fields.

His specific suggestions include ways to support young people and encourage them to follow God's call into those fields; how to influence television programming and encourage production of good literature; and how to encourage colleges to prepare people to be influential in those important fields. Since he is speaking about the areas we have called the "Megiddos" of culture, his book offers excellent, practical applications of this concept.

DATA FILE

Water Systems of Old Testament Times

Because Israel is an arid country, water has always been important to its inhabitants. In the ancient Near East, cities were built only where fresh water existed. People spent a good part of their day obtaining water for their needs.

When a city was small, a nearby spring, well, or cistern was sufficient. But as a city grew, its inhabitants took steps to protect their water supply from threatening armies. During Solomon's time, a wall or corridor often extended from the city wall to the nearby spring or well. But this setup was vulnerable to extended sieges.

During the late ninth or early eighth century B.C., a new technology emerged: the water shaft. People would dig a shaft to reach the water table and—sometimes using a horizontal tunnel, too— would direct the water into the city. During Hezekiah's reign, for example, a tunnel system allowed water from a spring outside Jerusalem to flow through the mountain ridge on which the city was built and into a pool inside the city walls.

The Entrance to the Water Shaft on Tel Megiddo

Scholars believe that sometime during the ninth century B.C., the inhabitants of Megiddo dug a square, vertical shaft more than 115 feet deep that connected to a horizontal tunnel. This tunnel traveled nearly 220 feet underneath the city to the cave in which a spring—the city's water source—was located. Evidently one crew began digging in the cave, the other at the bottom of the shaft inside the city. When the builders met in the middle, they had accomplished one of the engineering wonders of the world! The cave was then sealed from the outside, securing the water supply from enemy attack. Every day women descended the steps that wound around the outside walls of the shaft and walked through the tunnel to the spring.

The Ancient Wall Blocking the Cave of the Spring at Megiddo (Outside View)

The Water Tunnel of Megiddo

THE EVIDENCE OF TIME

How to Tell a Tel

Israel is a land of hills and mountains. In fact, a first-time visitor often is amazed by how little flat land there is. Most travelers also notice that Israel is dotted with a distinctive type of hill that has steep sides, a flat top, and looks a bit like a coffee table—especially when it is located in a valley and is viewed from above. Such a hill is called a *tel*, and tels are particularly important to Bible students.

A tel comprises layers and layers of ruined settlements that have been rebuilt on top of the ruins of previous settlements. In general terms, here's how tels such as Tel Megiddo were formed.

Stage 1

People settled on the site, eventually building a wall and gate. The king or rulers would build a palace and a temple, and the people would build houses inside the city walls. Often a steeply sloped rampart was built against the wall to protect the hill from erosion and to keep enemies away from the base of the wall. Over time, the ramparts were replaced or covered with others. These buried walls and ramparts gave the hill its steep, straight shape.

Stage 2

As the city grew and prospered, it became an attractive prize. Enemies would lay siege to it, sometimes penetrating the defenses and killing its inhabitants. Armies were usually brutally destructive in their conquests. Occasionally enemies remained to occupy the city, but usually they marched off, leaving behind smoking ruins.

Because of droughts, wars, or other reasons, once-prosperous cities were sometimes abandoned. Sand carried by the relentless winds of the Middle East gradually covered what remained of the houses and streets. Nomads would pitch their tents on the site, then move on. Soon the ruins blended into the landscape.

Stage 3

Even when a city was destroyed or vacated, the three conditions necessary for establishing a settlement in that place usually remained—a water source or adequate rainfall, an occupation that could generate a consistent food supply, and a defensible location. So, eventually people resettled on the same site. Lacking the heavy equipment needed to remove the debris left by previous inhabitants, the newcomers filled in holes, gathered larger building stones, leveled off the top of the hill, and rebuilt. Soon another prosperous community developed. Inevitably, its success attracted enemies . . . and the cycle of destruction and rebuilding resumed.

Tel Beth Shean

Stage 4

Over centuries—even millennia—layers upon layers of settlements accumulated (sort of like a layer cake), so the hill became higher and higher. Each layer—or stratum—records what life was like during the time of a particular settlement. Jerusalem has at least twenty-one layers, and Megiddo has even more. Locked within these layers are artifacts such as pottery, jewelry, weapons, documents, gates, temples, palaces, and houses—all of which are waiting for archaeologists to uncover their stories and discover how the people of those settlements lived.

Artifacts unearthed at Tel Megiddo and other tels enable us to know how people lived during biblical times: what they ate, how they worshiped, what their customs were, and many other important details. Each tel is, in effect, a unique gift from God that helps make ancient times more relevant to us today and helps us better understand the Bible's message.

FACT FILE

Three Essential Conditions

The environment of the Middle East, including Israel, is harsh and mostly unsuitable for settlement. For a location such as Megiddo to be habitable, three conditions were needed.

Fresh Water

Although rainfall is plentiful in some regions of Israel, most rain falls during the winter. During ancient times, many communities stored rainwater in cisterns. If rainfall was below average, cisterns dried up and people abandoned their city. If an enemy laid siege to a city, only the cisterns inside the city walls were available to the people, and the water often ran out, causing the city to fall. Jerusalem was built next to the spring of Gihon. The residents of Megiddo, Hazor, and Gezer dug tunnels through bedrock to reach fresh water. Without an abundant water supply, no settlement could grow.

Profitable Occupation

People needed the opportunity to either grow a consistent food supply or be able to buy food.

- Olive trees flourished in Judea and Galilee.
- Wheat grew in the valleys of Judea and the Valley of Jezreel.
- Shepherds raised sheep and goats in the wilderness.
- Chorazin and Ekron had large, olive-oil processing facilities.
- Jerusalem was famous for its purple dye.
- Some cities supplied travelers using the Via Maris, the major trade route through the country.

A Defensible Location

The political climate in the Middle East was volatile, so cities typically were built on hills ringing fertile valleys so the inhabitants could defend themselves. Jerusalem, for example, was initially built on a long, narrow hill and then spread across a valley and encompassed another hill. Azekah was situated on a hill overlooking the Elah Valley, the site of David's confrontation with Goliath.

who is god?

questions to think about

1. What kinds of situations can tempt us to lose faith in God and pursue other "gods" that we think will make our lives better?

2. Describe a situation in which you felt pulled between two opposing values and had a difficult time choosing one over the other. What did you feel? How did you eventually make your decision?

3. Think about a godly person you know who reflects God in everything he or she does. What about that person communicates that the Lord is God? What effect does that person have on others?

video notes

The Geographical Setting—Mount Carmel

The Historical Setting—King Ahab

Elijah—His Name, His Mission

The Confrontation on Mount Carmel

video Highlights

1. What effect did King Ahab's leadership have on the Israelites?

2. Why is the meaning of Elijah's name significant in light of his confrontation with the prophets of Baal on Mount Carmel?

3. What did the three-and-a-half-year-long drought communicate to the Israelites, whose faith was wavering between God and Baal? What is the significance of the fact that the drought ended after Elijah prayed?

4. What circumstances or responses of the people indicate that the Israelites were confused as to which god was the true God?

WHY MOUNT CARMEL?

Did you ever wonder why Elijah chose Mount Carmel as the place to confront the prophets of Baal and Asherah? Consider the following facts about Mount Carmel:

- It was more than 1,000 feet high and already had an altar (in bad repair) dedicated to God (1 Kings 18:30).
- It symbolized fertile splendor (Isaiah 35:1–2), typically receiving more than thirty inches of rain per year. (*Carmel* means "God's vineyard.")
- It was the most heavily forested area in Israel, making it an ideal place in which to show the Canaanite (who worshiped fertility gods) who really was the one true God.
- It was probably desolate after more than three years of drought, so the people knew that God, or perhaps Baal, was angry. This formerly lush site was a good illustration. (In other instances, Mount Carmel became withered as a result of curses. See Isaiah 33:9; Amos 1:2; and Nahum 1:4.)

The Valley of Jezreel

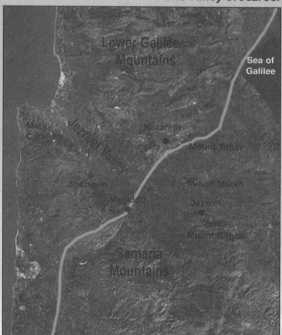

small Group Bible Discovery

Topic A: Israel's Growing Confusion About God

1. Shortly before his death, Joshua reviewed Israel's history, highlighting all that God had done for them. Then he asked the people of Israel to make a commitment to God. What was their response? (See Joshua 24:14–16, 22–25.)

2. What does 1 Kings 11:6–11 reveal about Solomon's commitment to follow God and the consequences of his decision?

3. What role did Jeroboam, the first king of the northern kingdom of Israel, play in leading the people away from God? (See 1 Kings 12:25–33.)

   a. What was God's response? (See 1 Kings 13:1–3, 33–34.)

b. Look up the following verses and note Jeroboam's legacy among future kings of Israel.

Reference	Legacy
1 Kings 16:25–26	
2 Kings 10:31	
2 Kings 13:1–2	
2 Kings 13:10–11	
2 Kings 14:23–24	
2 Kings 15:8–9	
2 Kings 15:17–18	
2 Kings 15:23–24	
1 Kings 16:29–33	

4. What impact did the kings' spiritual commitment have on the people of Israel? (See 1 Kings 18:17–21.)

THE TRUTH OF THE MATTER

During Ahab's reign, he and the Israelites tried to serve both Yahweh and Baal. Unwilling to commit to one or the other, they worshiped both. They would honor Yahweh, then go to high places to sacrifice to Baal, burn incense under Asherah poles, and participate in religious rites with prostitutes. Elijah challenged them to consider their actions—to consider the futility of trying to serve two masters—and to make a choice. He knew that the values represented by Baal and God were contradictory.

Jesus also addressed the importance of choosing whom to serve when He commented on the futility of serving both God and money: "No one can serve two masters. Either he will hate the one and love the other, or he will be devoted to the one and despise the other" (Matthew 6:24).

Topic B: The Role of God's Prophets

1. Through Moses, God promised that He would send prophets to help His people remain faithful to Him in a pagan world. These prophets would call people back to God's words and ways and communicate Yahweh's demand for total allegiance. Note what each of the following verses reveals about God's prophets.

    a. Deuteronomy 18:14

    b. Deuteronomy 18:15

    c. Deuteronomy 18:18

d. Deuteronomy 18:19

e. Deuteronomy 18:20

PROFILE OF FAITH

What Made Elijah Great?

It's easy to think that Elijah was morally or spiritually superior to us, but he wasn't. He was just like us. He had strengths and weaknesses, good days and bad days. As the following Scriptures illustrate, he needed correction, encouragement, and the knowledge that other believers were standing against Baal, too.

- 1 Kings 19:3–4
  Fearing for his life, Elijah ran into the Negev Desert. Ready to quit, he prayed for death.
- 1 Kings 19:7–8
  God answered Elijah's prayer and provided food and drink.
- 1 Kings 19:10
  Elijah confessed his despair, fear, and weakness to God.
- 1 Kings 19:11–13
  After sending a powerful wind, earthquake, and fire, God revealed Himself to Elijah through a whisper.
- 1 Kings 19:18
  God revealed to lonely Elijah the encouraging news that 7,000 Israelites had not bowed their knees to Baal.

What made Elijah great? He completely committed himself to God and doing what God wanted him to do!

2. What messages did God give to Elijah to give to Ahab? What was the purpose of those messages? How did Elijah know when to give them? (See 1 Kings 17:1–3; 18:1–2, 17–18.)

3. After God used Elijah to convict the Israelites of their sinfulness in worshiping Baal (1 Kings 18:39), one might think that Elijah would have had an easier life. But what happened soon afterward, and what does that reveal about the role of God's prophet? Read 1 Kings 19:1–4, 10.

Topic C: The Significance of Biblical Names

In biblical times, people understood that a name expressed the essence or identity of a person. A good name thus meant more than even a good reputation because it identified the character of its bearer.

1. The word *Elijah* is composed of two Hebrew words: *El*, which means "god," and is a general reference to deity; *Jah*, which is one part of the word *Yahweh* and represents the most holy name of God.

    a. Why is Elijah's name so significant in light of what he said to the Israelites in 1 Kings 18:21?

    b. How does what Elijah said in his prayer (1 Kings 18:36–37) relate to the meaning of his name?

2. What did God demonstrate when He changed Abram's name to Abraham (Genesis 17:1–5)? What did Pharaoh demonstrate when he renamed Joseph (Genesis 41:45)?

3. In the Near East, a person's name identified something about the person's character or circumstances (such as birth or family).

   a. Why did Sarah and Abraham name their son "Isaac," which means "he laughs"? (See Genesis 17:17.)

   b. Why did Moses receive his name, which meant "to draw out"? (See Exodus 2:1–10.)

4. In Matthew 1:20–21, we read that an angel told Joseph in a dream that his wife Mary would give birth to a son, and that he was to give the baby a specific name. What was this name, and why was it given?

5. When God told Moses, "I know you by name" (Exodus 33:17), what was He saying besides the fact that He recognizes us as individuals?

Topic D: "High Places"

1. God allowed His people to employ cultural practices and ideas if they had no pagan content and were used only in God's service. Since the people of the ancient Near East honored their gods by worshiping them on high places, God allowed His people to build altars to Him—and Him alone—on high places. He also communicated with His people on high places. The following verses will help you gain a picture of the appropriate use of high places.

Reference	High Place Events
Genesis 22:1–2, 9–14	
Exodus 19:20–22; 31:18	
Numbers 22:41; 23:1–5	
Deuteronomy 27:1–7; Joshua 8:30–31	
Judges 6:25–27	

(continued on page 60)

(continued from page 59)

Reference	High Place Events
1 Samuel 9:10–14	
1 Chronicles 21:18–26	
2 Chronicles 3:1	

The Temple Mount at Jerusalem

2. What did God tell the Israelites to do with the high places where the Canaanites worshiped? (See Deuteronomy 7:5; Numbers 33:52.)

3. The Israelites didn't follow God's commands concerning high places. What, in fact, did the Israelites do in the high places and what was the result? (See 2 Kings 17:6–12.)

The Altar at Megiddo

DATA FILE

The High Place and Altar at Dan

When Israel was divided into the northern kingdom (Israel) and the southern kingdom (Judah) in 920 B.C., the high place at Dan was established as a worship site in northern Israel. Archaeological evidence indicates that it:

- Measured sixty-two feet square.
- Was surrounded by a wall, with a staircase leading up to it.
- Had buildings on it that housed the shrine or "idol" that was worshiped there.

Three different high places were built on the same site.

(continued on page 62)

(continued from page 61)

Site 1

This site dates to King Jeroboam in the tenth century B.C., who—after Israel split into two parts—needed an alternative to the temple established by David and Solomon in Jerusalem. Jeroboam worshiped a golden calf on this site (1 Kings 12:26–30), which had a platform sixty feet long and twenty feet wide and an altar in front of the steps. Avraham Biran, the archaeologist directing this excavation, discovered that the fire that destroyed the shrine of Jeroboam had also turned the stones red.

Site 2

Someone, probably King Ahab, rebuilt the high place and made it larger. The Israelites continued to sink deeper into pagan practices and values.

Site 3

During the reign of Jeroboam II (ca. 760 B.C.), a large staircase and altar in front of this massive high place were added. Only parts of this altar, such as one of the horns that protruded from the four corners and part of the stairs leading to the altar, have been found.

During Jeroboam's reign, the prophet Amos predicted the final destruction of Israel because of its idolatry and pagan practices (Amos 3:12–15; 5:11–15; 8:14). Thirty years later, the brutal Assyrian army destroyed the northern ten tribes, who ceased to exist. Ashes and burn marks from a great fire on the altar and high place confirm Amos' prediction.

The High Place and Altar at Dan

Topic E: Ways in Which God Reveals That He Is God

1. What does God use in our world today to reveal that He is God? (See Isaiah 43:11–12.)

2. How did God prove Himself to Pharaoh? (See Exodus 7:17, 20.)

3. How did God prove Himself and His mighty power to "all the peoples of the earth"? (See Joshua 4:21–24.)

4. What did Solomon say in front of the entire assembly of Israel? (See 1 Kings 8:59–60.)

5. Why did David fight Goliath? (See 1 Samuel 17:45–47.)

6. What had God done to demonstrate Himself to the Canaanites, including Rahab, the prostitute who lived in Jericho? What was the effect? (See Joshua 2:8–11.)

7. What did Hezekiah pray after being challenged by the powerful Assyrian king? (See Isaiah 37:18–20.)

8. What did God do for Namaan to cause him to bless God? And what did Namaan affirm afterward? (See 2 Kings 5:13–15.)

faith lesson

Time for Reflection

Read the following passage of Scripture and take the next few minutes to consider who is Lord of your life.

> Then Elijah said to all the people, "Come here to me." They came to him, and he repaired the altar of the LORD, which was in ruins. Elijah took twelve stones, one for each of the tribes descended from Jacob, to whom the word of the LORD had come, saying, "Your name shall be Israel." With the stones he built an altar in the name of the LORD, and he dug a trench around it large enough to hold two seahs of seed. He arranged the wood, cut the bull into pieces and laid it on the wood. Then he said to them, "Fill four large jars with water and pour it on the offering and on the wood." "Do it again," he said, and they did it again. "Do it a third time," he ordered, and they did it the third time. The water ran down around the altar and even filled the trench. At the time of sacrifice, the prophet Elijah stepped forward and prayed: "O LORD, God of Abraham, Isaac and Israel, let it be known today that you are God in Israel and that I am your servant and have done all these things at your command. Answer me, O LORD, answer me, so these people will know that you, O LORD, are God, and that you are turning their hearts back again." Then the fire of the LORD fell and burned up the sacrifice, the wood, the stones and the soil, and also licked up the water in the trench. When all the people saw this, they fell prostrate and cried, "The LORD—he is God! The LORD—he is God!" Then Elijah commanded them, "Seize the prophets of Baal. Don't let anyone get away!" They seized them, and Elijah had them brought down to the Kishon Valley and slaughtered there.... Now Ahab told Jezebel everything Elijah had done and how he had killed all the prophets with the sword. So Jezebel sent a messenger to Elijah to say, "May the gods deal with me, be it ever so severely, if by this time tomorrow I do not make your life like that of one of them." Elijah was afraid and ran for his life.

1 KINGS 18:30–40; 19:1–3A

1. Just as Elijah's very identity was a testimony to his commitment to God, your identity can be built on God. How can you, in God's power, reveal the person and presence of God to other people?

2. What are the most significant "Baals" (evils) that lure people away from God in your culture today?

3. Which method(s) are most effective in bringing the power of God to bear against these evils?

4. What would God have you do—given your time, resources, opportunities—to call your culture to faith in God and lead others to godly obedience?

5. What might be the price of your commitment to reveal God to your culture?

Action Points

Take a few minutes to review the key points you explored today, then write down an action step (or steps) that you will commit to this week as a result of what you have learned.

1. *God demands that we recognize that He alone is Lord of our lives. He calls us to follow Him obediently and not to waver. We are to serve Him wholeheartedly and not to trust in other gods.*

    When Elijah challenged the Israelites to stop wavering between God and Baal, they were silent. Indeed, they didn't stand up for God until after He sent fire down from heaven that burned up Elijah's sacrifice and the altar on which it stood. In contrast, when Joshua challenged the Israelites years earlier to evaluate whom they would serve (Joshua 24:15), they resoundingly said that they would serve the Lord.

    In what ways do you waver between serving God completely and placing faith in something or someone else?

2. *When we live out who God has made us to be, people will see God.*

    Elijah, whose very name meant "Yahweh is God," did what God called him to do, and the people saw the evidence of God in a powerful way. When the Israelites recognized who God was, they renounced Baal and killed the prophets of Baal and Asherah.

    As people observe you in daily life—at home, at work, at play—what do they see? Do they see someone who is totally committed to God and following His ways? When

they see you, are they reminded of who God is . . .
whether or not they choose to follow Him?

What commitment are you willing to make to becoming
a modern "Elijah," a living witness of God's power and
presence who passionately reflects God in everything
you do?

The wages of sin

Questions to Think About

1. If you suddenly learned that God would send His judgment upon your culture—including the people who are following Him—within two years unless people turn back to Him, how would you live differently this week?

2. Which aspects of your culture do you think are most displeasing to God? Why are they an affront to Him?

video notes

Lachish—a Great City, a Terrible Fall

Sad history ... refused to follow ways of
the Lord.

2 Kings 17
well-fortified city...

God's Judgment at the Hand of the Assyrians

Siege of Lachish,

Hezekiah's Example

tore down asherah poles

Did what was right in
eyes of the Lord. Did all he
could to face future difficulties ...
prepared.

Angel of Lord killed Assyrians.

Our Mandate to Impact Culture

" You alone are God."

video Highlights

1. What did you learn through this video about the nature of the ongoing battle between good and evil?

2. Why did God allow the Assyrians to annihilate the ten tribes of Israel? *Whole culture went down because of the few who wronged.*

3. What did King Hezekiah do when challenged by the Assyrian king? *prepared*

4. Certainly many other righteous people before him had prayed to God for deliverance from the Assyrians, so why do you think God responded as He did to Hezekiah's prayer?

THE TRUTH OF THE MATTER

The Terrible Assyrians

Their empire was located in Mesopotamia near the Euphrates River.

The people had such a bad reputation that Jonah fled when God commanded him to speak to Nineveh, Assyria's capital (Jonah 1:1–3).

Known for their ruthlessness in battle and horrific treatment of captives, Assyrian soldiers were equipped with the latest weaponry—barbed arrows, catapults, and siege machines.

The Assyrian army inflicted maximum suffering on its enemies in order to intimidate people who might otherwise resist. (Only individuals who had certain skills or abilities might be spared.)

The Middle Eastern World

Assyrian kings took great pride in recording their military conquests in writing (on tablets, clay cylinders, and obelisks) and in pictorial reliefs on stone slabs lining palace walls. Along with a recounting of victories won and plunder taken, archaeologists have found chilling lists of how the Assyrians tortured their captives. These included:

- Flaying (cutting skin into strips and pulling it off a living victim)
- Beheading
- Impaling (inserting a sharpened stake beneath the rib cage of a living victim, putting the stake into the ground so it stood erect, and leaving the victim hanging until the stake pierced a vital organ causing the victim to die)
- Burning people (especially babies and children) alive
- Severing hands, feet, noses, ears, tongues, and testicles
- Gouging out eyes

ASSYRIA'S CONQUESTS

Circa 740 B.C. King Tiglath-Pileser began plundering Israel (2 Kings 15:29). He destroyed many cities, brutally killed their inhabitants, and left Israel with only the capital of Samaria intact.

Circa 735 B.C. King Shalmaneser marched on Samaria after Hoshea—the last king of Israel—refused to pay tribute to the Assyrians. The Assyrians marched on Samaria, slaughtered its inhabitants, and destroyed the remainder of the northern kingdom.

722 B.C. The ten northern tribes ceased to exist as a people. The Israelites who remained in Israel were forcibly mixed with other religious and ethnic groups and became the hated Samaritans of the New Testament. Those who were deported disappeared from history.

Circa 700 B.C. The new Assyrian king, Sennacherib, focused his attention on Judah, where he destroyed many cities. (He claimed to have destroyed forty-six walled cities and deported more than 200,000 captives.)

The Divided Kingdom

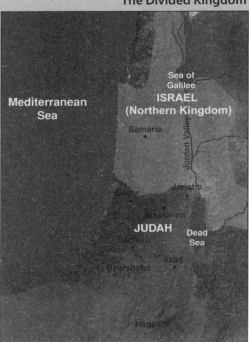

small Group Bible Discovery

Topic A: Guarding the Approaches to Jerusalem

The Israelites lived primarily in the mountains, clustered in towns surrounding Mount Moriah and the city of Jerusalem. After David established his kingdom, Jerusalem became the focal point of the Israelites' religion and their national identity. So, the city needed protection from the enemies of Israel.

1. According to the map of Israel on page 75, which key cities protected access routes to Jerusalem and thus had to be controlled?

2. Even before Jerusalem became the capital of Israel, the Israelites realized they needed to protect the territory surrounding it. Read 1 Samuel 13:23–14:1, 8–15 and note which approach to Jerusalem was threatened and who defended it. Refer to the map on page 75 to help you.

3. According to 1 Samuel 17:1–3, 48–52, where did the Philistines pitch camp? What happened to them after David killed Goliath?

4. From which direction did King Sennacherib of Assyria move his army toward Jerusalem? (See Isaiah 36:1–2.)

Topography of Israel

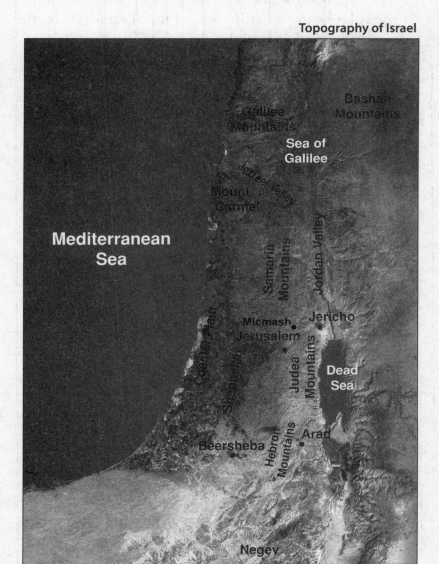

5. In the video, Ray Vander Laan pointed out, "It's safe to say that if Lachish stood, Jerusalem would stand; if it fell, Jerusalem would fall." Lachish was a strategic city because it was crucial to the defense of Jerusalem. The relationship between Lachish and Jerusalem illustrates a spiritual truth: we need to defend the less-central issues in order to protect the crucial beliefs and values of the Christian faith. In the chart below, identify some of the "Lachishs" and the "Jerusalems" of our culture.

The "Lachishs" The less-central issues that must be defended in order to protect the more crucial values	The "Jerusalems" The key beliefs and values of the Christian faith

EVIDENCE FILE

Tel Lachish: Its History Unfolds

Israel is dotted with a certain kind of hill called a *tel*. These hills have steep sides, flat tops, and look a bit like coffee tables. They are, in effect, comprised of layers and layers of settlements piled on top of each other. In Jeremiah 30:18, for example, we read about how Jerusalem will be "rebuilt on her ruins." Jeremiah 49:2 describes how Rabbah, an Ammonite city, will become "a mound of ruins."

In general terms, here's how Tel Lachish was formed:

Stage 1

People settled on the site, eventually building a wall and gate. Often a rampart was built against the wall to protect the hill from erosion and keep enemies away from the base of the wall.

Stage 2

The settlement was abandoned, due to war, drought, etc. Then the ruins faded into the landscape.

Stage 3

People moved back to the same spot, filled in holes, gathered larger building stones, leveled off the hill, and rebuilt. Then the city's success attracted enemies . . . and the cycle of destruction continued.

(continued on page 78)

Tel Lachish

(continued from page 77)

Stage 4

Layers upon layers accumulated (sort of like a layer cake), so the hill became higher. Each layer—or stratum—records what life was like during a particular time. Artifacts discovered in the *tel* reveal a great deal about how people lived during particular times.

Tel Lachish—the main setting of this video—reveals the city's rich history. First settled more than 4,000 years before Jesus' birth, it was destroyed and rebuilt at least six times. Between these total destructions, various changes in civilization occurred. For example, the layer of Hezekiah's time (700 B.C.) reveals massive fortification towers, a huge gate complex, and a palace. Another layer contains the remains of the city's fiery destruction (587 B.C.).

Tel Lachish—and other tels—help us to better understand the Bible's message. Each tel is, in effect, a unique gift from God to help us better understand His Word. The insights we gain help us to better understand and interpret the Bible's message.

CONFIRMING EVIDENCE

The Palace of a Great King

Assyria's kings were committed to more than military conquest. As part of their religious duty, they also constructed massive public buildings. Sennacherib, for example, built a new palace that he named the Palace Without a Rival. His records indicate that the labor force that built it was composed of deportees from many conquered nations (probably including Israel).

This palace, which was discovered during the late nineteenth century, contained more than seventy halls and chambers, all of them lined with stone panels (called *reliefs*) that depicted Sennacherib's accomplishments. Enormous statues of winged bulls guarded the doors of the hallway that led to the main chamber. Hallway walls were lined with panels commemorating the destruction of the cities of Judah, including the siege of Lachish.

Topic B: The Judgment of God

God is incredibly patient with His people, always ready to forgive. But when they are repeatedly rebellious and refuse to heed His warnings, He will send judgment.

1. What cautions did God give the Israelites soon after they entered Canaan? (See Deuteronomy 8:11–20.)

2. What did God promise would happen if the Israelites failed to obey Him? (See Deuteronomy 28:15, 21–22, 49–52, 62–63.)

3. Which sins did the Israelites commit that finally brought God's judgment? (See 2 Kings 17:9–17.)

4. After Israel was divided, God sent His prophets to both Israel and Judah. Look up the following verses and take note of the message each prophet delivered.

Jeremiah 1:14–16	The Prophet	
	The Kingdom	
	The Message	
Hosea 10:1–2, 5–10	The Prophet	
	The Kingdom	
	The Message	

5. What did God allow the Assyrians to do to Israel because of their failure to keep His commandments? (See 2 Kings 17:18–23.)

WORTH OBSERVING

God Punishes People for Their Sins

The biblical reality that God hates sin and will eventually punish it is reinforced in the stories of the Flood, Sodom and Gomorrah, the conquest of Canaan, and the exile of the Israelites.

God's Judgment

God made the Sabbath principle central to His creation. As part of their recognition that God owned everything, the Israelites were to set apart the seventh day for the Lord. To violate the Sabbath day was a serious sin because it denied God's sovereignty. Also, every seventh year the land was to lie fallow and not be farmed (Leviticus 25:1–7). Yahweh promised to provide an abundant crop in the sixth year so no one would be hungry during the following year.

But the Israelites' illicit affair with pagan gods started almost as soon as they arrived in Canaan. Because idolatry did not acknowledge Him as the one true God, God condemned it. He knew that idol worshipers would work on the Sabbath day because they would not recognize that they belonged to God and that God owned the land. So He told them, in Leviticus 26:35, that if they continued to be disobedient He would take their land from them so it would "have the rest it did not have during the sabbaths you lived in it."

The Israelites' continued disobedience finally caused God to bring judgment on them. (See 2 Kings 17:18–20 and 2 Chronicles 36:15–20.) He ripped His stiff-necked people from their land, asserting His ownership over it and them (2 Chronicles 36:21). In 722 B.C., the Assyrians destroyed the people of Israel (the northern ten tribes). In 586 B.C., the people of Judah were exiled to Babylon for seventy years—and the land rested for seventy years.

The Hope Promised

Although God allowed Assyria to take the people of Judah into exile, He did not forsake His people, nor did He end His plan for their redemption. Second Chronicles 36:22–23 ends with optimism because the Israelites would return to their land and the temple would be rebuilt.

As it turned out, God's people experienced tremendous spiritual growth during the Babylonian Captivity (586 B.C.). Without their temple, the Israelites learned that obedience is better than sacrifice (Psalm 40:6 and Isaiah 1:10–20). They learned the importance of obeying all of God's commands or suffering the consequences. The Israelites returned from Babylon with a renewed focus on God and the need to be faithful to Him (Ezra 9:10–15). Never again would Baal worship and the shedding of innocent blood be the religion of the nation.

Topic C: Four Kings Who Prolonged God's Patience

In 722 B.C., the ten northern tribes of Israel were destroyed when God punished them for forsaking Him. The southern kingdom of Judah, however, continued to exist for more than a century before receiving God's judgment at the hands of the Babylonians. Why did Judah last so much longer than Israel? Consider the work of several, God-fearing kings who brought the people of Judah back—at least temporarily—from the brink of disaster.

King Asa

1. What did King Asa do that pleased God? What was the result? (See 2 Chronicles 14:2–7.)

2. What did God promise King Asa, through the prophet Azariah? (See 2 Chronicles 15:1–2.)

3. In what ways did King Asa encourage his people to seek the Lord? (See 2 Chronicles 15:8–16.)

4. What was King Asa's great act of foolishness later in his life? How did God respond? (See 2 Chronicles 16:1–9.)

King Joash

5. What did King Joash do to turn the people back toward God? (See 2 Chronicles 24:8–9, 12–14.)

6. What did King Joash do after the death of Jehoiada, the chief priest? What was the result? (See 2 Chronicles 24:17–21, 23–25.)

King Hezekiah

7. How would you describe Hezekiah's spiritual insight and commitment to God? (See 2 Chronicles 29:1–10.)

8. What did Hezekiah do to restore the people's relationship with Yahweh? What were the results? (See 2 Chronicles 29:3–5, 20–24, 35–36; 31:1.)

King Josiah

9. Instead of following false gods, what did King Josiah do? What was the result? (See 2 Chronicles 34:3–8, 14, 21–33.)

Topic D: Hezekiah—Prepared to Defend God's People

1. According to 2 Chronicles 31:20–21, how did God respond to Hezekiah's faithfulness?

2. Although Hezekiah had undertaken one of the greatest religious reforms the nation of Israel had ever seen, God still judged the culture for its sinfulness. What did God allow to happen? (See 2 Chronicles 32:1, 9.)

3. After Sennacherib, Assyria's king, invaded Judah with plans to attack the fortified cities of Judah, what plans did Hezekiah implement? How did he encourage his people? (See 2 Chronicles 32:2–8.)

4. How did Sennacherib respond to Hezekiah and the Israelites' God? (See 2 Chronicles 32:9–19 and Isaiah 36:12–18.)

5. What was Hezekiah's response to Sennacherib's challenges and mockery? (See Isaiah 37:1, 14–20.)

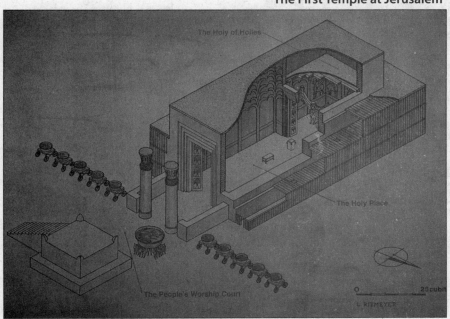

The First Temple at Jerusalem

6. How did God respond to Hezekiah's prayer? (Isaiah 37:21–22a, 33–37)

DATA FILE

Hezekiah's Amazing Water System

The spring of Gihon, which flowed out of a cave on the eastern side of the hill on which Jerusalem was built, provided the city's main water supply. (More than 24,250 cubic feet of water per day still flow from it.) As long as the cave's entrance was outside the city walls, the city's water supply was vulnerable to disruption by enemies.

Before David captured the city in about 1000 B.C., the Jebusites living there dug a shaft from the city into the cave. Quite possibly Joab, David's commander, captured the city by entering the cave and climbing up the shaft. (See 2 Samuel 5:8 and 1 Chronicles 11:6.)

Jerusalem of David and Solomon

Although Hezekiah trusted God totally (Isaiah 37:14–20), he resolved to do everything possible to prepare his people to face the Assyrians. When he heard about the Assyrians' arrival, he ordered his workers to dig a tunnel from the cave through the ridge on which the city was built in order to bring water to the western side of the ridge—to the pool of Siloam within the city walls. Then he covered up the cave's opening (2 Kings 20:20; 2 Chronicles 32:2–4). Today, this extraordinary accomplishment—built more than 700 years before Jesus walked on the earth—still ranks as one of the engineering marvels of the ancient world. Here's why:

- Two teams of workmen, working from both directions, chiseled a tunnel barely two feet wide through solid rock, sometimes at points more than 150 feet underground, and met in the middle. And they did this without modern tools or instruments!

- The tunnel is 1,748 feet long and has a drop of just 12 inches.
- Water more than waist deep still flows through the tunnel.
- In 1880, boys playing in the tunnel discovered writing chiseled into the ceiling. Called the Siloam Inscription, it describes the dramatic moment when the two teams of workers met. Today, the inscription is in the Istanbul Archaeological Museum, having been removed from the tunnel when the Turks ruled Palestine during the late nineteenth century.

Hezekiah's Water Tunnel

faith Lesson

Time for Reflection

Read the following passage of Scripture and take the next few minutes to consider how God deals with a culture that refuses to obey Him.

> Zedekiah was twenty-one years old when he became king, and he reigned in Jerusalem eleven years. He did evil in the eyes of the LORD his God and did not humble himself before Jeremiah the prophet, who spoke the word of the LORD. He also rebelled against King Nebuchadnezzar, who had made him take an oath in God's name. He became stiff-necked and hardened his heart and would not turn to the LORD, the God of Israel. Furthermore, all the leaders of the priests and the people became more and more unfaithful, following all the detestable practices of the nations and defiling the temple of the LORD, which he had consecrated in Jerusalem. The LORD, the God of their fathers, sent word to them through his messengers again and again, because he had pity on his people and on his dwelling place. But they mocked God's messengers, despised his words and scoffed at his prophets until the wrath of the LORD was aroused against his people and there was no remedy. He brought up against them the king of the Babylonians, who killed their young men with the sword in the sanctuary, and spared neither young man nor young woman, old man or aged. God handed all of them over to Nebuchadnezzar. . . . until the seventy years were completed in fulfillment of the word of the LORD spoken by Jeremiah.

> 2 CHRONICLES 36:11–17, 21

1. In what ways has your knowledge of God—His hatred of sin, His willingness to forgive, His judgment—changed as a result of this study?

2. Which issues today may not seem terribly important, yet must be defended in order to protect the more crucial values?

3. Just as the people of Israel and Judah descended into unfaithfulness by taking small steps, so Christians today find themselves becoming unfaithful to God in small but significant ways. In what way(s) have you taken small steps away from God? What were (or are) the consequences?

4. To follow God faithfully, you must be willing to destroy any "high places" (sinful practices, habits, and "gods") to which you are devoted. Which "high place" in your life needs to be confronted and destroyed?

Action Points

Take a moment to review the key points you explored today, then jot down an action step (or steps) that you will commit to this week as a result of what you have learned.

1. *When a culture fails to live out its God-given calling and disobeys the standards found in His Word, God may send judgment on the entire culture—those who are godly as well as those who persist in wrongdoing.*

For generations, Israel and Judah disobeyed God repeatedly even though He kept calling them back to Himself. They persisted in idol worship and refused to commit themselves to Him and to the lifestyle He requires. So God finally sent judgment in the form of the Assyrian army.

For which particular sins might God choose to judge your entire culture if it remains unrepentant?

2. *It is God's desire that those who love Him make an impact on their culture. Those who are wholly devoted to God and are willing to stand against evil can be very effective in redeeming the culture.*

Because of Hezekiah's faithful devotion to God, he was able to impact his culture in godly ways and ultimately helped to bring about God's purposes in the world—Jesus' lineage through the tribe of Judah. At the heart of his effectiveness was the fact that Hezekiah did what was right, prepared for the difficulties to come while trusting God completely, and truly desired that the world would know that God is God.

In what specific way(s) are you—like the people of Lachish—content to absorb the sinful values of secular society instead of standing firm for God, trusting Him, and being His instrument in your world?

What specific steps might God be calling you to take in order to impact your culture for Him, so that the world will continue to know that God is God?

The Lord is My shepherd

Questions to Think About

1. Which words would you use to describe the character of God?

2. Which images or metaphors would you use to complete the sentence: God is like _____?

video notes

Discovering the Wilderness

Shepherds and Their Sheep

Jesus—Our Good Shepherd

The Judea Wilderness

video нighlights

1. Place yourself in the setting of this video. Imagine what it would be like to be a Bedouin shepherd living in the wilderness—no electricity, no running water, no telephone or television, no neighborhood supermarket with its assortment of fresh produce. How might such a lifestyle change your perception of and need for God?

2. In what ways did Ray Vander Laan's explanation of what "green pastures" in the Negev really are surprise you?

The Northern Edge of the Wilderness

3. What is meant by the term "undershepherd"? In what ways are you an undershepherd who leads other people?

4. Why is it so dangerous for sheep to drink from water located in wadis? How does this image parallel what people do today to quench their spiritual thirst?

Wilderness Pasture

Quiet Waters in the Wilderness

FOR GREATER UNDERSTANDING

Word Pictures of the Scriptures

The early writers and readers of the Scriptures viewed their world in concrete, not abstract, terms. So they used word pictures and symbolic actions rather than formal definitions to describe God and His relationship with His people. Note what the following word pictures reveal about God and our relationship to Him.

John 6:35a	Jesus, the "bread of life," offers spiritual food that will completely satisfy our hunger. He alone offers the spiritual truth that provides life.
John 8:12	Jesus is the "light of the world." He will provide spiritual light for anyone who follows Him, so instead of stumbling in spiritual darkness His followers will be able to follow a clearly lit path.
Psalm 18:2	God is our "rock." He is steadfast, immovable, a sure place on which to stand and take refuge. God is our "fortress," a place of safety. God is our "deliverer" who saves us. He is our "shield" who protects us from harm. He is the "horn," a symbol of strength, of our salvation.
Isaiah 40:11	God is presented as a loving "shepherd." He takes care of His people like a loving shepherd cares for his or her flock. Even the weak and defenseless are secure in His tender care.
Psalm 100:3	God's people are portrayed as the "sheep" of God's pasture, meaning they will receive daily protection and sustenance from Him.
John 3:3	Jesus used the term "born again" to illustrate the spiritual changes that occur when a person accepts Him as Lord and Savior. This word picture reflects the completely new person God creates through His salvation—a person who sees God's kingdom in a new light, a person who has a new hope, new goals, and a new understanding of spiritual truth.

small group bible discovery

Topic A: The Lessons of the Wilderness

The Israelites traversed the wilderness before entering the Promised Land, and their wilderness experience transformed them, as it did a number of leaders of God's people. Let's look at the role the wilderness played in the Israelites' lives.

1. Under what circumstances did Israel's forefathers spend time in the desert before God called them to accomplish His mission for their lives? How did God use these men?

   a. Genesis 12:1–10; 13:1–4

   b. Exodus 2:11–22; 3:1–4, 7–10

   c. 1 Samuel 23:12–15; 2 Samuel 2:1–4

The Northern Edge of the Wilderness

2. Biblical writers understood that while His people were in
    the desert, God nurtured and disciplined them so they
    would learn to depend solely on Him. Read Psalm 78:12–
    29 and note what God did to nurture their faith in Him.

3. Of what did King David remind the Israelites? Which
    images did he use to make his point? (See Psalm 95:6–11.)

4. Through the prophetic words of Jeremiah, what did God
    say to the Israelites in Canaan? (See Jeremiah 2:1–7.)

5. What did God, through Moses, say to the people as they
    were preparing to enter the Promised Land? (See
    Deuteronomy 8:1–6, 10–18.)

DATA FILE

The Wilderness of Israel

Much of Israel is rugged desert. The two most significant wilderness areas in Israel are the Judea Wilderness to the east and the Negev to the south. These deserts contain more rock than sand, are mountainous in spots, and receive just enough rainfall during winter months to sustain nomadic shepherds and their flocks.

The Judea Wilderness

The Judea Mountains form the middle section of the central mountain range in Israel. On the eastern side of this mountain ridge, descending into the Great Rift Valley more than 1,300 feet below sea level, is the rocky wasteland of Judah. Little rain falls here, and the land is split by deep wadis formed by centuries of rain runoff. Because this wilderness borders fertile mountain ridges for more than fifty miles, villages such as Bethlehem were able to sustain both shepherds (like David) and farmers (like Boaz and Ruth). Shepherds lived on the desert's fringes; farmers worked the soil of the mountains.

The Negev

The arid Negev (Negev means "dry") lies south of the Hebron Mountains that form the southern section of Israel's central mountain range. This desert receives fewer than eight inches of rainfall annually in the north and less than half that amount in the south. Except for a few settlements that use modern methods to catch rain runoff, only nomads live here.

Because the wilderness was so close to settled areas, many people seeking solitude or safety from authorities hid there. For example, in the Negev David hid from Saul (1 Samuel 26), John the Baptist isolated himself from religious practices of the day (Matthew 3), and Jesus faced the devil (Matthew 4). People also associated the wilderness with the coming of the Messiah. Isaiah 40:3b reads, "In the desert prepare the way for the LORD; make straight in the wilderness a highway for our God."

The northern region of the Negev, from the Hebron Mountains to the Zin Wilderness, is good sheep country. Its rolling hills surround large, broad valleys such as the Valley of Beersheba in which Abraham settled.

The Negev's central region is rugged and cut by deep canyons in the Zin Wilderness. Because the climate and terrain are so inhospitable—even to nomads—at least one scholar has suggested that the "valley of the shadow of death" mentioned in Psalm 23 may refer to the canyons here. The southern portion of the Negev is called the Wilderness of Paran in the Bible. This region is the most barren of all.

The Judea Wilderness

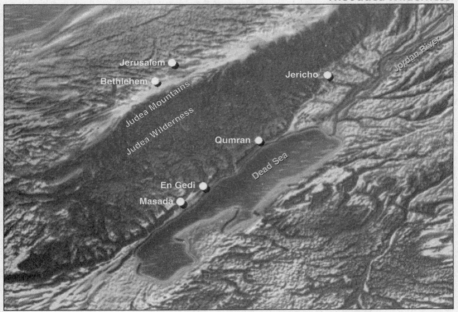

Topic B: "The Shepherd"

The shepherd image appears more than 200 times in the Bible, including more than 15 times in the New Testament. Knowing that the Israelites, as shepherds, would clearly understand the relationship of the shepherd and his sheep, God used it to illustrate His relationship with His people.

1. What do the images of the shepherd and his sheep in the following verses reveal about God and His people?

   Isaiah 40:10–11

   Psalm 95:6–7

   Psalm 78:51–54

   Psalm 100:3

   Luke 12:22–32

   Luke 15:3–7

   John 10:14–16

FACTS TO PONDER

The Myth of Green Pastures

Although we might think that the "green pastures" David mentioned in Psalm 23 refer to tall, lush grasslands like those in North America and other locations, the truth is that such grasslands don't exist in Israel. The regions in Israel where shepherds live have two seasons: the rainy season from November through March (when even the desert becomes green), and the dry season from April through October when the landscape is brown. Even during the rainy season, the grasses remain short. Sheep that graze in the marginal areas of the wilderness receive enough nourishment for the moment ... but no more. Day to day, the sheep depend on their shepherd to lead them to the food and water they need.

In Exodus 16:4–5, 13–18, we read that God—the Good Shepherd—provided bread and quail from heaven for His people every day. The Israelites were to take what they needed for that day ... and no more. But some people took too much to make sure they'd have some the next day (Exodus 16:20). When that happened, the food they tried to store became full of maggots and smelled awful.

Knowing that each of us has the tendency to worry about the future, Jesus shared how important it is for us to trust God to meet our needs every day. He taught that we should seek God and His righteousness and trust Him to meet our needs today ... and then to trust Him tomorrow in the same way. "Therefore," He said, "do not worry about tomorrow" (Matthew 6:34; see also 6:25–33).

Topic C: A Promise Made in the Wilderness

Because of our sinful nature, we often pursue our desires instead of God's will. But God is patient and faithful. When we fail to do His bidding, God often provides another opportunity to obey Him and fulfill His plan. Consider how God used the Israelites' experience with the Amalekites to teach His people the crucial importance of obedience.

1. What did the Amalekites do, and what did God promise to do to them? (See Exodus 17:8–14.)

2. What did God command the Israelites to do? (See Deuteronomy 25:17–19.)

3. What did God, through Samuel, tell King Saul to do? (See 1 Samuel 15:1–4.)

4. What did King Saul do in response to God's command? (See 1 Samuel 15:7–9, 20–25.) What was God's response?

5. About 400 years after Saul's disobedience and death, how did a descendant of Agag, Haman, endanger the entire nation of Israel? (See Esther 3:1–6, 8–11.)

PROFILE OF A PEOPLE

The Israelites in the Wilderness

After God miraculously delivered the Israelites from Egyptian bondage, they wandered through the Negev and the Sinai Wilderness. When they reached the northern edge of the Negev, the Israelites sent spies into Canaan. Upon learning about giants and huge fortified cities, the people became afraid and refused to enter the Promised Land. Because of their disobedience and lack of faith, God commanded them to remain in the wilderness—"the vast and dreadful desert" (Deuteronomy 8:15)—for forty years, one year for each day the spies had been gone.

During these desert years, God taught His people faith and trust, preparing them to live obediently in the Promised Land *so that the world would know that He was God*. He also disciplined them for their lack of faith, disobedience, and complaining. Moses recorded that God humbled the Israelites so that they would learn to depend on Him for everything, because "man does not live on bread alone but on every word that comes from the mouth of the LORD" (Deuteronomy 8:3).

For obvious reasons, their forty-year wilderness wanderings significantly impacted the Israelites. Various Bible references emphasize the lessons they learned:

- The Psalmist reminded the Israelites of God's faithful love in the wilderness (Psalm 105:38–45; 107:4–9).
- The Psalmist warned the Israelites against repeating their earlier sins (Psalm 81:11–16; 78:14–40).
- Jeremiah reminded the Israelites of what God had done for them and how they had disobeyed Him and disregarded His warnings (Jeremiah 2:5–8; 7:21–26).
- Micah reminded them of God's previous blessings (Micah 6:3–5).
- The writer of Hebrews used the Israelites' wilderness wandering as an illustration of unbelief (Hebrews 3:7–19).
- Paul summarized some of the Israelites' sins in the wilderness and reminded readers to be careful (1 Corinthians 10:1–13).

(continued on page 104)

(continued from page 103)

- Jesus, when He faced the tempter, used the lessons of the wilderness to defeat him. (See Matthew 4:4 and Deuteronomy 8:3;
  Matthew 4:7 and Deuteronomy 6:16.)

Today, the wilderness imagery of the Bible refers to our lives here on
earth as we prepare for our "promised land" in heaven. It portrays difficult
times in our lives when we learn to trust God. It offers a picture of God
disciplining us for our sins and reminds us of the Messiah's eventual
return. Truly the wilderness is still the place where we—God's people—
learn that we cannot live on bread alone.

6. What opportunity did God, in His mercy, give to Esther, a
    descendant of Kish, Saul's father? (See 1 Samuel 9:1–2;
    Esther 2:5–11, 16–17; 4:12–17; 7:1–6, 9–10.)

7. How do the prophetic words of Mordecai, Esther's uncle,
    relate to what God may be calling us to do and be in our
    unique circumstances? (See Esther 4:12–16.)

Topic D: Undershepherds

Some scholars believe that the practice of young shepherds tending sheep under the watchful eyes of adults is the basis for the biblical picture of God—the Chief Shepherd—appointing undershepherds to care for His flock.

1. What does 1 Samuel 16:10–13 reveal about the son of Jesse whom God had chosen to be king of Israel?

2. What happened to the undershepherds who cared for their father's flock in Midian? (See Exodus 2:16–17.)

3. What terminology did Jesus use to give Peter the responsibility to care for His flock? (See John 21:15–17.)

4. Whom did God condemn in Ezekiel 34:1–10? Why? What imagery did God use to make His point?

5. After the undershepherds of Israel failed in their God-given responsibilities, what did God promise to do? (See Ezekiel 34:11–16.)

6. What imagery did Paul use when speaking to the Ephesian elders, and what did he tell them to do? (See Acts 20:28–31.)

7. What did God promise to do to the shepherds who had not cared for the sheep He had entrusted to them? (See Jeremiah 23:1–4.) And what did He promise to do for the sheep?

8. What guidelines did God, through Peter's writing, give to undershepherds who cared for His people? What did God promise would happen when Jesus—the "Chief Shepherd"—appears? (See 1 Peter 5:2–4.)

Topic E: The Chief Shepherd—Committed to Leading His Sheep

1. Whereas shepherds in the Western world use dogs to drive their sheep ahead of them, shepherds in the Middle East *lead* their sheep. Look up the following Scriptures and discover how God led the Israelites out of Egypt.

   Psalm 78:51–53

   Exodus 13:20–22

2. As a result of God's leadership, what would the Israelites receive? (See Isaiah 49:8–10.)

3. To what did Jesus compare His relationship to His followers? What sacrifice was He willing to make for them? (See John 10:11–14.)

4. What does Matthew 18:12–14 reveal about God the Shepherd and His commitment to His sheep?

5. How did God use the imagery of sheep to communicate what had happened to His people? (See Jeremiah 50:6, 17–19.)

DATA FILE

The Wadis of Israel

The wilderness of Israel is scarred by deep, riverbed canyons called *wadis* (Hebrew, *nahal*). Although the wilderness in Israel receives little rainfall, the central mountains receive a great deal of moisture during the winter months. The thin topsoil of the mountains cannot absorb all this water, which runs into the valleys to the west and runs through the wadis into the desert wilderness areas that lie to the east and south.

The runoff is so great that the wadis quickly fill with raging torrents. The water rushes down and roars through the wadis, cutting deep walls into them and sweeping away any animals or people in its path. These flash floods can occur even when the sky is clear because the rains fall some distance away. Even today, these floods pose a great danger to shepherds and their sheep.

Wadis both hinder and help the shepherds. On one hand, crossing the wadis is difficult and can be very dangerous. Sheep, which are undiscerning, will choose to walk in dangerous water. That's why the shepherd

A Wadi in the Negev

Flood in the Wadi

must *lead* the sheep. But the flash floods that crash through the dry canyons leave behind quiet, refreshing pools that enable vegetation to grow and provide watering places for sheep. It is the shepherd's task to determine if these pools are safe for the flock to drink from and lie beside—if they are the "quiet waters" referred to in Psalm 23:2.

faith Lesson

Time for Reflection

Read the following passage of Scripture and take the next few minutes to reflect on the significance of the wilderness and the role of the Good Shepherd in your life.

> The LORD is my shepherd, I shall not be in want.
> He makes me lie down in green pastures,
> he leads me beside quiet waters,
> he restores my soul.
> He guides me in paths of righteousness
> for his name's sake.
> Even though I walk
> through the valley of the shadow of death,
> I will fear no evil, for you are with me;
> your rod and your staff, they comfort me.
> You prepare a table before me
> in the presence of my enemies.
> You anoint my head with oil;
> my cup overflows.
> Surely goodness and love will follow me
> all the days of my life,
> and I will dwell in the house of the LORD
> forever.

PSALM 23

1. What brought hope to the psalmist as he faced the challenges of his life?

2. What brings hope to your life?

3. In light of what you learned in this session about what the "green pastures" in Israel are really like, how do you view the provision God gives you *today* and what He promises to provide for you *tomorrow*?

Water from Rock

This psalm is so familiar that it's easy to overlook the profound message it expresses. Take a few minutes to meditate on this psalm and personalize it:

1. What does your Shepherd provide for you so that you do not want?

2. What are the green pastures and quiet waters of your life?

3. In what ways does He restore your soul?

4. Identify the paths of righteousness into which He leads you for *His* sake.

5. What is the valley of the shadow of death that strikes fear into your heart?

6. In what ways does God comfort you?

7. Describe the feast He has prepared for you in the sight of your enemies.

8. How have you felt His anointing?

9. In what ways does your cup overflow?

10. What assurance do you have that you will dwell in the house of the Lord forever?

Action Points

Take a moment to review the key points you explored today, then jot down an action step (or steps) that you will commit to this week as a result of what you have learned.

1. *Jesus is our Good Shepherd; we are His sheep.* In much the same way that the shepherds of Israel's wilderness lead, protect, and nourish their flocks, Jesus will lead us to green pastures and provide us with what we need for today. He will walk before us, inviting us to follow Him and to model His actions as we interact with other people and influence our culture. He will lead us to quiet water—places of safety where we can be refreshed.

   Do you live as if Jesus is your good Shepherd? In what practical ways do you see Him leading and caring for you?

   What commitment are you willing to make to follow His leading?

2. *Sometimes life is difficult and can be compared to the vast wilderness areas of ancient Israel. Things are parched . . . confusing . . . and dangerous.* But God is our Shepherd—even in the wilderness. In fact, as we learn to trust Him and faithfully follow Him through the wilderness, the roots of our faith will grow strong.

   Think about a "wilderness" in which you have lived—or maybe are living today. What lessons did you learn

through God's provision and guidance for you during that wilderness experience?

In what ways are you living in light of those lessons today?

In what ways do you need to remember what God did for you then?

What will you do to cultivate your ability to hear your Shepherd's voice in your wilderness?

god with us

questions to think about

1. What do the Ten Commandments signify to you? What was God's purpose for writing them?

2. How can we know that God is real? What evidence of His presence can we see today?

video notes

Arad and Its Temple

God's Covenant:

With Abraham

Moses and the Ten Commandments

Jesus, the Covenant Sacrifice

God's Dwelling Place Today

video нighlights

1. What do you observe about the location of Arad on the map on page 118? Why do you think the people built a temple there?

2. Why do you think God made specific covenants with Abraham and later with His people through Moses on Mount Sinai?

Tel Arad

3. How has learning about God's purpose for writing the Ten
    Commandments—to summarize His covenant and remind
    the Israelites of His love—changed how you view them?

The Divided Kingdom

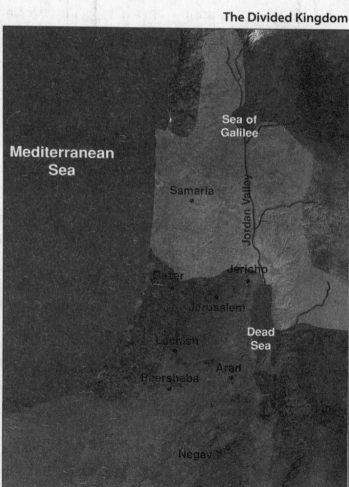

4. In light of the fact that the ark of the covenant in the temple was truly the dwelling place of God, what difference should it make that Christian believers are now the temples of God?

COMPELLING EVIDENCE

Arad's God-fearing People

Archaeologists at Arad, who believe the inhabitants who lived there nearly 3,000 years ago worshiped only *Yahweh*, have discovered the following items:

- Potsherds with writing on them (*ostraca*) inscribed with the names of priests mentioned in the Bible and Yahwistic names (that contain part of God's name).
- Bowls inscribed "Sons of Bezalel." (See Exodus 31:1–11.)
- An offering bowl inscribed "Sacred for the Priests."
- A temple similar in design to Solomon's temple in Jerusalem.

The Temple at Arad

The Holy of Holies
The Holy Place
The People's Worship Court

small group Bible Discovery

Topic A: Sacrifices in the Temple

1. In ancient Israel, what did the animal sacrifices made on the temple altar signify? (See Leviticus 17:5–7, 11; Hebrews 9:22.)

2. According to God's command, what daily sacrifices were the Israelites to make? (See Numbers 28:1–8.)

The Outer Court of the Temple at Arad

3. Describe the guidelines that God gave for the temple altar, which was to stand in the outer worship court. (See Exodus 20:25–26; 27:1.)

4. Describe the location and purpose of the bronze Sea. (See Exodus 30:17–21. Note: The bronze Sea of Solomon's temple is described in 2 Chronicles 4:2–5.)

5. Which imagery found in Acts 22:14–16 and 1 Corinthians 6:11 is similar in function to the bronze Sea?

DATA FILE

The Temple Courts

The temple in Arad was built in a style probably influenced by Egyptian architecture and with materials similar to those used to build the average Israelite house. The temple in Jerusalem, on the other hand, was elaborately furnished and followed the Phoenician-Syrian temple design. Yet both temples contained the same courts and accomplished the same worship functions.

The Holy of Holies

(God's dwelling place) in Jerusalem contained the ark of the covenant, which held the tablets of the covenant (the Ten Commandments). In the temple in Arad, this area was reached by climbing two steps—symbolizing going up to God. Two standing stones were found in the temple in Arad. These stones may have represented the tablets of the Ten Commandments—God's covenant with Israel.

The Holy Place

(Priests' court) was a rectangular room between the worship court and the Holy of Holies that contained the table of showbread, golden lampstand, and the altar of incense. (The temple in Arad had two altars; the temple in Jerusalem had one.) The showbread was placed as an offering in the presence of God (Leviticus 24:5–9). This offering symbolized a thanksgiving gift to God as well as a request for His provision of food. The priests, on behalf of the people, ate the bread as a symbol of their relationship with God.

At Arad, the Holy Place was positioned so that its longest walls opened to the Worship Court on one side and the Holy of Holies on the other. (See the diagram of the two temples on page 123.) This style brought the people in the Worship Court closer to the priest in his room and to God in the Holy of Holies. So the room was called the "broad room."

In the temple in Jerusalem, the Holy Place's shortest walls bordered the Holy of Holies and the Worship Court, so the people were farther away from the priest and from God in the Holy of Holies. So the room was called the "long room."

The Worship Court

(The people's place) a large outer court in which the people stood to worship, contained the altar of sacrifice and the laver or basin (the bronze Sea).

The Temples at Arad and Jerusalem

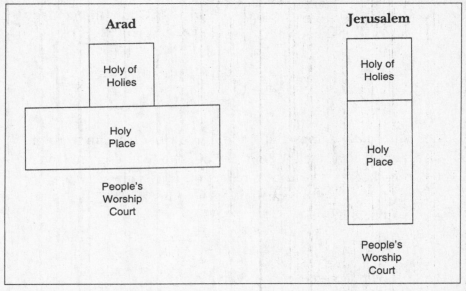

Panarama of the Temple at Arad

Topic B: The Holy Places of the Temple

The altar and bronze Sea were positioned in the people's worship area of the temple. The temple also had a Holy Place for the priests, and the Holy of Holies, which was God's place. Note the purpose for the furnishings in these courts of the temple.

1. Describe the table of showbread that God commanded Moses to make. (See Exodus 25:23–30.)

2. The golden lampstand stood in the Holy Place in front of the veil covering the Holy of Holies and represented God's presence. It was to be a reflection of His glory. How was the lampstand to be made? (See Exodus 25:31–32, 37–40; Numbers 8:3–4.)

3. During which hours of the day were the priests to keep the oil lamps on the lampstand burning? (See Exodus 27:20–21.)

4. How many of these lampstands did Solomon make for the first temple in Jerusalem? (See 2 Chronicles 4:7.)

The First Temple at Jerusalem

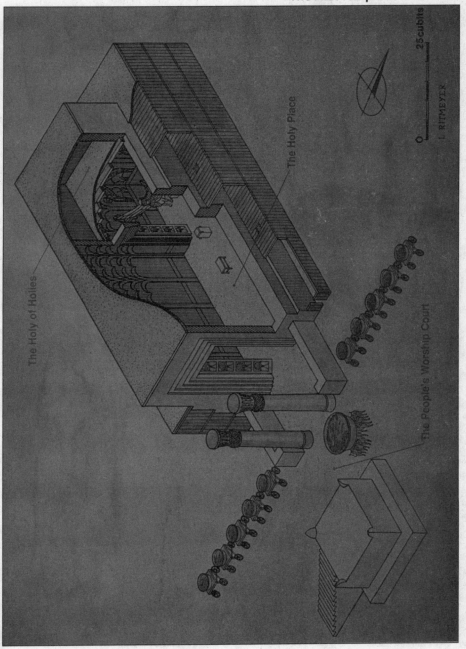

5. The altar of incense was located in front of the entrance to the Holy of Holies. The temple in Jerusalem had one altar of incense; the temple in Arad had two. What is the significance of the offering of incense? (See Exodus 30:7–8; Psalm 141:2; Revelation 5:8.)

The Holy Place of the Temple at Arad

6. The ark of the covenant, which became the focus of God's presence among His people (Psalm 99:1), was kept in the Holy of Holies. Who was allowed into the Holy of Holies, and under what circumstances? (See Leviticus 16:2, 34. Note: Leviticus 16 specifies in detail the activities of the Day of Atonement.)

DID YOU KNOW?
Rather than choosing a unique design for His temple in Jerusalem, God chose a well-known, older design that followed the Phoenician-Syrian temple design. Huram-Abi, the man Hiram, king of Tyre, sent to Solomon to supervise construction of the temple, was well skilled in this design style. In fact, Scripture reveals that he was "trained to work in gold and silver, bronze and iron, stone and wood, and with purple and blue and crimson yarn and fine linen" (2 Chronicles 2:14). He also was an expert engraver!

Topic C: God's Covenants with His People

In the ancient Near East, there was a special covenant form in which a greater party (often a king) established a relationship with a lesser party (often a vassal). The greater party determined the responsibilities of each, and the lesser party accepted or rejected the relationship. God used this kind of covenant when dealing with His people.

1. The following verses each represent a covenant God made with people. For each, note (1) the person through whom God made the covenant; (2) why God, as the superior party, had the right to make the covenant; (3) what God promised within the relationship; and (4) any sign given as a symbol of the covenant.

The Covenant	God's Right	God's Promise	The Sign
Genesis 9:8–17			
Genesis 15:4–21; 17:1–11			

(continued on page 128)

(continued from page 127)

The Covenant	God's Right	God's Promise	The Sign
Exodus 19:3–6; 24:3–8, 12; 31:18; 40:20–21			
2 Samuel 7:1–26			
Hebrews 13:20; Luke 22:19–20; 1 Corinthians 5:7			

DATA FILE

The Ark of the Covenant

- Was uniquely designed by God before any other sacred object (Exodus 25:10–22).
- Was made of acacia wood commonly found in the Sinai Peninsula.
- Was three feet nine inches long, two feet three inches wide, and two feet three inches high.
- Had gold plating and a golden rim around the top.
- Stood on four legs.
- Contained two gold rings on each side so the Levites—the priestly tribe—could insert poles into it and carry it.
- Had a cover (the mercy seat or atonement seat) made of pure gold.
- Two cherubim—probably sphinxes with wings outstretched—were positioned on top of the lid. They expressed the people's longing to feel safe in God's sheltering arms. The ark assured them that the holy God of Abraham was sovereign over all things and was a protecting, forgiving presence in their lives. (See 1 Chronicles 28:2 and Psalm 99:1.)

SURPRISE!

Traditionally, Christians have believed there were two tablets of the Law: one tablet (commandments 1–4) describing what our relationship with God should be; the other (commandments 5–10) describing what our relationship with other members of the covenant should be.

Although it is correct to divide the commandments into these two categories, nothing in Scripture supports the idea of two partial tablets. Everything we know about Israelite culture points to all ten commandments being written on each tablet. God gave both copies to Moses because God's sacred place and Moses' sacred place were the same: the ark of the covenant.

Topic D: Jesus, the Sacrifice for Our Sins

1. Hundreds of years before Jesus, what did the prophet Isaiah say that Jesus would do for us? (See Isaiah 53:4–6, 11–12.)

2. What terminology did John the Baptist use to describe Jesus? (See John 1:29.)

3. What is Jesus called in 1 Corinthians 5:7?

4. In light of the terminology used in the two Scripture references above, what is the significance of the specific time at which Jesus died on the cross? (See Matthew 27:46–50.)

5. What does Hebrews 9:11–14 reveal about Jesus the Messiah's impact on the Israelites' central act of worship—blood sacrifices?

6. After both temples were destroyed, Jewish followers of Yahweh pointed to passages like Micah 6:6–8 to indicate that obedience to God is the "new" sacrifice. How is that passage similar to Romans 12:1?

DATA FILE

The Preparation for Jesus' Coming—Fulfillment of a Promise

God's covenant with Abraham demonstrated the *promise of God*. He declared His commitment to the Israelites by walking the blood path to make a covenant with Abraham and his descendants.

Through the tabernacle, ark of the covenant, and temple, God's people experienced the *presence of God*. God began restoring His presence among His people.

The tablets of the Ten Commandments sealed the *relationship between the people and their God*.

Although these commitments spectacularly demonstrated God's love, they anticipated an even greater act of love: the birth of God's own Son. The person of Jesus would fulfill everything that had come before. God would walk with His people, as He had walked with Adam and Eve. The blood of Jesus the Lamb would atone for the sins of those who believed in Him. In Jesus, God would reaffirm His dedication to the covenant relationship He made with His servant Abraham.

In Jesus, God fulfilled the promise He made to the Hebrews of giving His own life to seal the covenant He had made with them. For this reason, Jesus could say, "Do not think that I have come to abolish the Law or the Prophets; I have not come to abolish them but to fulfill them" (Matthew 5:17).

God's choice of the covenant to describe His relationship with His people highlights the degree of His love for us. Not only did the great sovereign Creator of heaven and earth descend to be in relationship with sinful human beings, He offered His life to provide escape for the very people who would violate His covenant! People of the ancient Near East cultures understood what a covenant was and recognized the indescribable gift of relationship God had given to those who believed in Him. It should be no less for us.

Topic E: God's Presence in the World

1. How near to His creation was God when He first created the world? What changed? (See Genesis 3:8, 23–24.)

2. What does Genesis 11:1–5 reveal about God's concern for His world?

3. What was the main purpose of the temple in Jerusalem? (See 2 Chronicles 5:7; 7:1–3.)

4. What happened to God's presence because of Israel's unbelief? (See Ezekiel 10:18–19.)

5. How did God restore His presence among His people? (See John 1:1, 14.)

6. In what way does God choose to reveal His presence today? (See 1 Corinthians 3:16–17.)

PROVOCATIVE EVIDENCE

Where God Dwells

The Scriptures reveal some remarkable parallels between God's home in heaven and His former home on earth in the temple in Jerusalem:

Heaven	Temple
God's dwelling place (2 Chronicles 6:21)	God's dwelling place (2 Chronicles 6:1–2)
God surrounded by cherubim (Revelation 4:6b–8; Ezekiel 1:6,10)	God surrounded by figures of cherubim (2 Chronicles 3:10–13)
God surrounded by His heavenly hosts (Revelation 5:11)	God surrounded by His earthly hosts (Numbers 2)
God is seated on a throne (Revelation 4:2–5)	The ark is God's throne (Psalm 99:1)
Altar representing the blood of the saints (Revelation 6:9)	Blood is sprinkled on the altar (Leviticus 1:10–11)
Prayers of the saints viewed as incense (Revelation 5:8)	Priest met with God at the altar of incense (Exodus 30:1,6)
Sea of crystal (Revelation 4:6)	Sea of bronze (1 Kings 7:23)

ꜰaith ʟesson

Time for Reflection

Read the following passage of Scripture and take the next few minutes to consider how God would have you view your covenant with Him.

And God spoke all these words: "I am the LORD your God, who brought you out of Egypt, out of the land of slavery. You shall have no other gods before me. You shall not make for yourself an idol in the form of anything in heaven above or on the earth beneath or in the waters below. You shall not bow down to them or worship them; for I, the LORD your God, am a jealous God, punishing the children for the sin of the fathers to the third and fourth generation of those who hate me, but showing love to a thousand [generations] of those who love me and keep my commandments. You shall not misuse the name of the LORD your God, for the LORD will not hold anyone guiltless who misuses his name. Remember the Sabbath day by keeping it holy. Six days you shall labor and do all your work, but the seventh day is a Sabbath to the LORD your God. On it you shall not do any work, neither you, nor your son or daughter, nor your manservant or maidservant, nor your animals, nor the alien within your gates. For in six days the LORD made the heavens and the earth, the sea, and all that is in them, but he rested on the seventh day. Therefore the LORD blessed the Sabbath day and made it holy. "Honor your father and your mother, so that you may live long in the land the LORD your God is giving you. You shall not murder. You shall not commit adultery. You shall not steal. You shall not give false testimony against your neighbor. You shall not covet your neighbor's house. You shall not covet your neighbor's wife, or his manservant or maidservant, his ox or donkey, or anything that belongs to your neighbor." When the people saw the thunder and lightning and heard the trumpet and saw the mountain in smoke, they trembled with fear. They stayed at a distance and said to Moses, "Speak to us yourself and we will listen. But do not have God speak to us or we will die." Moses said to the people, "Do not be afraid. God has come to test you, so that the fear of God will be with you to keep you from sinning."

EXODUS 20:1–20

1. How does your view of the Ten Commandments change when you read it as a statement of God's love and commitment to you rather than just a list of dos and don'ts?

2. What does it mean to you that God was willing to shed His own blood and die in order to pay for your violation of His covenant?

3. You are to your world what the ark of the covenant and the temple were to Israel—God's dwelling place. How, then, should you live so that the world may know that He is God?

4. The people of Arad left a God-fearing legacy behind. Looking back on your life, how do you think people will remember you? Which of your possessions testify to your faith in God? Which don't?

Action Points

Review the key points you explored today, then jot down an action step (or steps) that you will commit to this week as a result of what you have learned.

1. *God has chosen to reveal His presence to the world through His people.* During Old Testament times, God made a binding covenant with His people that was summarized on each of the two stone tablets He gave to Moses on Mount Sinai. To further emphasize His love and His desire to be with His people, God chose to live on the ark of the covenant in which the stone tablets were stored. The ark of the covenant, which was placed in the Holy of Holies in the temple, was literally God's dwelling place on earth.

   Thus the Ten Commandments, which were written on each of the two stone tablets, were far more than a checklist of God's requirements. They were a reminder of the covenant God had made with His people. The tablets said, in effect, "I am God. I love you enough to make a covenant with you through My own blood."

   What in your life reminds you of God's deep love for you and His ongoing commitment to you?

2. *When the temple in Jerusalem was destroyed, God's presence left the earth until He revealed it again through Jesus, His beloved Son.* In Jesus, God fulfilled the promise He had made to Abraham of giving His own life to seal the covenant He had made. Not only did the sovereign Creator live among sinful human beings to demonstrate His presence, He offered His life to save those who had broken His covenant.

3. *Through Jesus' blood that was shed on the cross for our sins,
    God created a new covenant in which we—those who have
    accepted Jesus the Messiah as our Lord and Savior—have
    become His temple.* As we live in relationship with Him,
    we make His presence known to a spiritually needy world.

    **What do people see when they see you? In what way(s)
    are you revealing God's presence and power to a watch-
    ing world?**

    **What will you do this week to more effectively present
    the reality of God's presence to the world around you? Be
    specific!**

DATA FILE

Covenant Forms

Ancient Near Eastern covenants, especially those between unequal parties, formed complex relationships. Many factors had to be considered:
the right of the greater party to make the covenant, obligations of each
party, penalties and benefits of the relationship, and the relationship's
history. So, covenantal documents were usually quite long. God's
covenant with Israel through Moses, for example, is recorded in the
Torah—the first five books of the Bible. God's covenant with believers in
Jesus is described in all sixty-six books of the Bible.

Covenants were carefully recorded and preserved. They were to be
read regularly and always obeyed. Moses, for example, wrote down the
words of God's covenant with His people in the Torah and commanded
that it be read every seven years (Deuteronomy 31:9–13, 24–26). The

(continued on page 138)

(continued from page 137)

summary document—the Ten Commandments—was stored in the most sacred place: the ark of the covenant, God's earthly throne.

In order to make sense of covenants, people followed a certain pattern that governed the materials contained in a covenant, including its content and form. A summary document representing the entirety of the relationship and following the accepted form of a covenant document was also provided.

Keeping in mind that God cut covenants as the superior party so that He alone determined their content, let's briefly review the components of the covenant God made with the Israelites.

The Preamble

It identified the two parties of the covenant. In the Torah, God established the identities of the parties in the creation story. He was the Creator, and Israel was His creation. In the covenant summary (the Ten Commandments), He said simply, "I am the LORD your God" (Exodus 20:2).

The Historical Prologue

The history leading to the cutting of the covenant was recited to prove the right of the superior party to make it. In the Ten Commandments, for example, the summary is simply, "... who brought you out of Egypt, out of the land of slavery" (Exodus 20:2).

Requirements (Commandments)

The Torah contains 613 of the requirements God placed on the people with whom He was in relationship. He placed even more obligations on Himself. In summarizing the commandments, these requirements were simplified to ten (Exodus 20:3–17). Some scholars have noted that Jesus reduced His summary to just two obligations (Matthew 22:37–40).

Blessings and Curses

Keeping a covenant brought specific rewards, and breaking it brought specific penalties. The Torah, for example, contains many blessings and curses.

The Summary Document

The short summary document, which could be easily read and stored, summarized the entire covenant and so represented the total relationship between the parties. Normally in Near Eastern culture, two summary documents were made; each party kept one in a sacred place. So, it seems clear that each tablet of the Ten Commandments contained all of the commandments. One copy was God's, and the other belonged to the people of Israel. Part of the purpose of the ark of the covenant was to hold the Ten Commandments, the summary of God's covenant with His people.

Additional Resources

History

Connolly, Peter. *Living in the Time of Jesus of Nazareth.* Tel Aviv: Steimatzky, 1983.

Ward, Kaari. *Jesus and His Times.* New York: Reader's Digest, 1987.

Whiston, William, trans. *The Works of Josephus: Complete and Unabridged.* Peabody, Mass.: Hendrikson Publishers, 1987.

Wood, Leon. Revised by David O'Brien. *A Survey of Israel's History.* Grand Rapids: Zondervan, 1986.

Jewish Roots of Christianity

Stern, David H. *Jewish New Testament Commentary.* Clarksville, Md.: Jewish New Testament Publications, 1992.

Wilson, Marvin R. *Our Father Abraham: Jewish Roots of the Christian Faith.* Grand Rapids: Eerdmans, 1986.

Young, Brad H. *Jesus the Jewish Theologian.* Peabody, Mass.: Hendrickson Publishers, 1995.

Geography

Beitzel, Barry J. *The Moody Atlas of Bible Lands.* Chicago: Moody Press, 1993.

Gardner, Joseph L. *Reader's Digest Atlas of the Bible.* New York: Reader's Digest, 1993.

General Background

Alexander, David, and Pat Alexander, eds. *Eerdmans' Handbook to the Bible.* Grand Rapids: Eerdmans, 1983.

Butler, Trent C., ed. *Holman Bible Dictionary.* Nashville: Holman Bible Publishers, 1991.

Edersheim, Alfred. *The Life and Times of Jesus the Messiah.* Peabody, Mass.: Hendrickson Publishers, 1994.

Archaeological Background

Charlesworth, James H. *Jesus Within Judaism: New Light from Exciting Archaeological Discoveries.* New York: Doubleday, 1988.

Finegan, Jack. *The Archaeology of the New Testament: The Life of Jesus and the Beginning of the Early Church.* Princeton: Princeton University Press, 1978.

Mazar, Amihai. *Archaeology of the Land of the Bible: 10,000–586 B.C.E.* New York: Doubleday, 1990.

To learn more about the specific backgrounds of the fourth set of videos, consult the following resources:

Avigad, Nahman. "Jerusalem in Flames—The Burnt House Captures a Moment in Time." *Biblical Archaeology Review* (November–December 1983).

Barkey, Gabriel. "The Garden Tomb—Was Jesus Buried Here?" *Biblical Archaeology Review* (March–April 1986).

Ben Dov, Meir. "Herod's Mighty Temple Mount." *Biblical Archaeology Review* (November–December 1986).

Bivin, David. "The Miraculous Catch." *Jerusalem Perspective* (March–April 1992).

Burrell, Barbara, Kathryn Gleason, and Ehud Netzer. "Uncovering Herod's Seaside Palace." *Biblical Archaeology Review* (May–June 1993).

Edersheim, Alfred. *The Temple.* London: James Clarke & Co., 1959.

Edwards, William D., Wesley J. Gabel, and Floyd E. Hosmer. "On the Physical Death of Jesus Christ." *Journal of American Medical Association (JAMA)* (March 21, 1986).

Flusser, David. "To Bury Caiaphas, Not to Praise Him." *Jerusalem Perspective* (July–October 1991).

Greenhut, Zvi. "Burial Cave of the Caiaphas Family." *Biblical Archaeology Review* (September–October 1992).

Hareuveni, Nogah. *Nature in Our Biblical Heritage.* Kiryat Ono, Israel: Neot Kedumim, Ltd., 1980.

Hepper, F. Nigel. *Baker Encyclopedia of Bible Plants: Flowers and Trees, Fruits and Vegetables, Ecology.* Ed. by J. Gordon Melton. Grand Rapids: Baker, 1993.

"The 'High Priest' of the Jewish Quarter." *Biblical Archaeology Review* (May–June 1992).

Hirschfeld, Yizhar, and Giora Solar. "Sumptuous Roman Baths Uncovered Near Sea of Galilee." *Biblical Archaeology Review* (November–December 1984).

Hohlfelder, Robert L. "Caesarea Maritima: Herod the Great's City on the Sea." *National Geographic* (February 1987).

Holum, Kenneth G. *King Herod's Dream: Caesarea on the Sea.* New York: W. W. Norton, 1988.

Mazar, Benjamin. "Excavations Near Temple Mount Reveal Splendors of Herodian Jerusalem." *Biblical Archaeology Review* (July–August 1980).

Nun, Mendel. *Ancient Stone Anchors and Net Sinkers from the Sea of Galilee.* Israel: Kibbutz Ein Gev, 1993. (Also available from *Jerusalem Perspective.*)

_____. "Fish, Storms, and a Boat." *Jerusalem Perspective* (March–April 1990).

_____. "The Kingdom of Heaven Is Like a Seine." *Jerusalem Perspective* (November–December 1989).

_____. "Net Upon the Waters: Fish and Fishermen in Jesus' Time." *Biblical Archaeology Review* (November–December 1993).

_____. *The Sea of Galilee and Its Fishermen in the New Testament.* Israel: Kibbutz Ein Gev, 1993. (Also available from *Jerusalem Perspective.*)

Pileggi, David. "A Life on the Kinneret." *Jerusalem Perspective* (November–December 1989).

Pixner, Bargil. *With Jesus Through Galilee According to the Fifth Gospel.* Rosh Pina, Israel: Corazin Publishing, 1992.

Pope, Marvin, H. "Hosanna: What It Really Means." *Bible Review* (April 1988).

Riech, Ronny. "Ossuary Inscriptions from the Caiaphas Tomb." *Jerusalem Perspective* (July–October 1991).

_____. "Six Stone Water Jars." *Jerusalem Perspective* (July–September 1995).

Ritmeyer, Kathleen. "A Pilgrim's Journey." *Biblical Archaeology Review* (November–December 1989).

Ritmeyer, Kathleen, and Leen Ritmeyer. "Reconstructing Herod's Temple Mount in Jerusalem." *Biblical Archaeology Review* (November–December 1989).

_____. "Reconstructing the Triple Gate." *Biblical Archaeology Review* (November–December 1989).

Ritmeyer, Leen. "The Ark of the Covenant: Where It Stood in Solomon's Temple." *Biblical Archaeology Review* (January–February 1996).

_____. "Quarrying and Transporting Stones for Herod's Temple Mount." *Biblical Archaeology Review* (November–December 1989).

Sarna, Nahum M. *The JPS Torah Commentary: Exodus.* New York: Jewish Publication Society, 1991.

"Sea of Galilee Museum Opens Its Doors." *Jerusalem Perspective* (July–September 1995).

Shanks, Hershel. "Excavating in the Shadow of the Temple Mount." *Biblical Archaeology Review* (November–December 1986).

"Shavuot." *Encyclopedia Judaica,* Volume 14. Jerusalem: Keter Publishing House, 1980.

Stern, David. *Jewish New Testament Commentary.* Clarksville, Md.: Jewish New Testament Publications, 1992.

Taylor, Joan E. "The Garden of Gethsemane." *Biblical Archaeology Review* (July–August 1995).

Tzaferis, Vassilios. "Crucifixion—The Archaeological Evidence." *Biblical Archaeology Review* (January–February 1985).

_____. "A Pilgrimage to the Site of the Swine Miracle." *Biblical Archaeology Review* (March–April 1989).

_____. "Susita." *Biblical Archaeology Review* (September–October 1990).

Vann, Lindley. "Herod's Harbor Construction Recovered Underwater." *Biblical Archaeology Review* (May–June 1983).

FAITH LESSONS VIDEO SERIES

Ray Vander Laan

Filmed on location in Israel, **Faith Lessons** is a unique video series that brings God's Word to life with astounding relevance. By weaving together the Bible's fascinating historical, cultural, religious, and geographical contexts, teacher and historian Ray Vander Laan reveals keen insights into Scripture's significance for modern believers.

> *"Nothing has opened and illuminated the Scriptures for me quite like the Faith Lessons series."* —Dr. James Dobson

Faith Lessons on the Promised Land, Crossroads of the World: Volume One 0-310-67864-1
Faith Lessons on the Prophets & Kings of Israel: Volume Two 0-310-67865-X
Faith Lessons on the Life & Ministry of the Messiah: Volume Three 0-310-67866-8
Faith Lessons on the Death & Resurrection of the Messiah: Volume Four 0-310-67867-6

JESUS

An Interactive Journey

Now, through the cutting-edge technology of interactive CD-ROM, you can make an incredible voyage—back to the life and times of Jesus! This exciting multimedia adventure takes you there, giving you an entirely new appreciation for the fascinating historical, geographical, and cultural backdrop that will enhance your understanding of the Gospel.

The high technology and vast amount of material in this unique presentation will captivate you for hours, while providing a solid understanding of the Gospel and its relevance to today's believer. It's great for personal and family Bible study, Christian schools, and a wide variety of church uses.

Compatible with Windows® 95 and Windows® 3.1

CD-ROM 0-310-67888-9

ECHOES OF HIS PRESENCE

Ray Vander Laan

Through historically accurate, fictional stories of people Jesus touched, *Echoes of His Presence* spans the gap between the history of Jewish tradition and the nature of Western thinking, making the Savior's ministry relevant, significant, and more meaningful than ever to today's believers. You'll understand Scripture in its cultural context . . . and you'll fall in love with Jesus all over again.

Hardcover 0-310-67886-2
Audio 0-310-67887-0

ZondervanPublishingHouse
Grand Rapids, Michigan
http://www.zondervan.com

A Division of HarperCollinsPublishers